THE ECOMMERCE GROWTH GAP

THE ECOMMERCE GROWTH GAP

Why Brands Get Stuck and the Operating System for Profitable, Predictable eCommerce Growth

JASON PAWLOSKI

Published by Baywood Press
New York, New York
publishing@baywoodpress.com

The Ecommerce Growth Gap, Jason Pawloski —1st ed.

"I've interviewed thousands of eCommerce executives, and the gap between what brands think they need and what actually drives performance is enormous. This book closes that gap. It's the clearest, most practical operating manual for eCommerce I've seen. If every CEO and eCommerce leader would read this, my job would be a lot easier, and a lot more brands would be successful."

—Harry Joiner, founder, eCommerceRecruiter.com

"Jason earned every insight in these pages the hard way. I've watched him do the work, learn the lessons, and turn hard-won experience into a system others can use. This book will help you close the Growth Gap that's been holding you back."

—Chris Johnson, chief digital officer, Allstate

"This book explains eCommerce in a way leadership teams can understand, govern, and scale. I've seen Jason close the Growth Gap more than once, in different businesses, with different teams and different challenges. This isn't luck. It's a repeatable approach."

—Trip Randall, president and CEO, Superfeet

CONTENTS

FOREWORD

by Chris Johnson
Chief Digital Officer, Allstate

I've worked with many talented operators over the years, but Jason stood out early, not just for his technical depth but for his insistence on understanding how things *actually* worked.

When we worked together at the global footwear company Wolverine Worldwide, he already had the ability to untangle systems, rebuild broken processes, and bring order to complexity. What he was still developing was the broader commercial lens, the understanding that eCommerce isn't a collection of tools or tactics but a business system that lives and dies by the profit and loss statement (P&L).

So I spent a fair amount of time reminding him of two truths he now quotes back to me: "Just follow the math," and "If this were easy, we wouldn't need to be here."

To his credit, he listened. More importantly, he learned. He learned how to connect acquisition, conversion, retention, merchandising, operations, and finance into a single system. He learned how to separate symptoms from causes. And he learned how to stay calm under pressure, even when the pressure was coming from me.

What impressed me most wasn't how quickly he picked up on things. It was how quickly he learned to simplify complexity. Jason could take a tangle of metrics, tools, incentives, and competing priorities and turn it into something an entire organization could actually act on. That combination of clarity, cross-functional fluency, and executional discipline is rare. It's also exactly what most digital organizations are missing.

Because the truth is, eCommerce has only gotten harder. Customer acquisition is more expensive. Dashboards are noisier. Expectations are higher. Patience is thinner, especially in the boardroom.

Many brands are doing more digital work than ever while producing weaker financial outcomes. The gap between eCommerce potential and performance has widened. Jason names that gap clearly. He also explains why it exists and, more importantly, how to close it.

This book doesn't offer secret tactics or flashy trends. It focuses on the system, the economics, operating discipline, and leadership behaviors that actually determine performance. It captures the mental models and patterns that the best operators rely on but rarely write down.

It's written for CEOs, boards, and investors who need clarity and for eCommerce leaders who need a blueprint they can actually run.

Jason earned every insight in these pages the hard way. I've watched him do the work, learn the lessons, and turn hard-won experience into a system others can use. If you're willing to see your eCommerce business clearly and lead it as the system it truly is, this book will help you close the Growth Gap that's been holding you back.

FOREWORD

by Trip Randall
President and CEO, Superfeet

I've spent my career leading consumer brands through growth, disruption, and reinvention. At Nike, we were building eCommerce capabilities before most of the industry understood what was coming. Later, at Sound United and Superfeet, the challenge was more familiar: significant potential sitting just out of reach, teams working hard but not always in the right direction, and leadership trying to make sense of growing complexity.

It was in that environment that I first worked with Jason Pawloski.

At Denon, Jason walked into a complex eCommerce business, absorbed an extraordinary amount of information in a short period of time, and surfaced the real story with a level of clarity I was not expecting. His diagnosis of our Growth Gap was fast, sharp, and complete. Not just what was happening but why, and what needed to change.

I remember finishing our review, closing the laptop, and telling him quietly, "You should do this for a living."

What stood out was not just his strategic thinking but his ability to connect brand, consumer behavior, and economics into a single operating model. He wasn't treating eCommerce like a marketing channel. He was treating it like a business.

When I later became CEO of Superfeet and we reached our own eCommerce inflection point, I didn't need to shop for partners. I knew exactly whom to call.

What Jason helped us do was not a marketing exercise or a technology overhaul. It was the disciplined work of turning eCommerce into a real operating system. One grounded in economics, aligned across functions, and understood by leadership.

The results were unmistakable. Revenue accelerated. Contribution margin strengthened. eCommerce penetration increased meaningfully. But the more important shift was internal. The organization gained clarity. Leadership and the board had confidence. Teams stopped reacting and started executing. The noise faded, and the system clicked.

I've now seen Jason create that outcome more than once, in different businesses, with different teams and different challenges. This isn't luck. It's a repeatable approach.

This book captures that approach. It explains eCommerce in a way that leadership teams can understand, govern, and scale. If you are responsible for growth, profitability, or enterprise value, you will recognize the patterns in these pages. More importantly, you will recognize the path forward.

HOW TO READ THIS BOOK

This is not a "growth hacks" book, a collection of channel-optimization tips, or a book designed to find small and incremental improvements within a broken model. This book was created to help you view your eCommerce business as a system. If you read it expecting to find shortcuts or smoking guns, you will be frustrated. However, if you read it to determine why the brand's effort, spending, and talent have not produced sustained, profitable growth, it will fundamentally change how you think about both eCommerce growth and leadership.

The book is deliberately organized into three parts.

Part 1 defines the eCommerce Growth Gap and explains why so many brands experience stalled growth despite increased spending, the adoption of new tools, and additional hiring. This is a diagnostic exercise, not an indictment.

Part 2 provides a detailed explanation of the root causes. The Five Forces describe the specific system failures that create and widen the Growth Gap. Each force compounds the others and must be addressed in sequence. Addressing them out of sequence undermines the diagnostic process.

Part 3 shows how healthy systems operate. This part of the book transitions from diagnosing issues to designing actionable solutions and implementing operational shifts to address them. It describes how strategy, economics, ownership, infrastructure, and demand converge to create a functioning system capable of producing consistent results.

Each chapter adds a layer. The full picture comes into focus as the holistic system takes shape.

The eCommerce Growth Gap Digital Toolkit

A companion toolkit is available to support your work as you read. It includes downloadable versions of the scorecards, templates, and road map tools referenced throughout the book. You will find it at toolkit.ecommercegrowthgap.com. The toolkit is most useful starting in Part 3, but it is worth knowing it exists before you begin.

How to Approach the Book Based on Your Role

While the book is structured as a journey, different types of leaders will face varying levels of pressure and may need to approach it differently.

CEOs/Board Members

Start with Part 1 to ensure alignment regarding the definition of the eCommerce Growth Gap. Utilize the CEO briefings provided at the end of each chapter to identify the strategic implications. If any of the briefings create discomfort, there is likely a failure within the system. Read that chapter in its entirety.

eCommerce Operators

Read the book sequentially. There is an intentional flow of logic from economics to capabilities to infrastructure to demand. Take special note of the operator diagnostics. These questions are designed to expose gaps and stimulate new ways of thinking that operational execution often masks.

Using What You Learn

Use what you learn to look for signals, not comfort. Identify which of the Five Forces seems most familiar or most defensible. The primary constraint is likely to reside within that area. Use the diagnostics to honestly assess your current reality, not to validate previous decisions. Making decisions based on an incomplete diagnosis is how the Growth Gap gets worse. Over time, utilize the language of this book as a common reference point among all levels of leadership (marketing, finance, operations). Once a team uses the same system terminology, decision-making becomes more clear, trade-offs become more apparent, and the sense of fragility in achieving growth diminishes.

The goal is predictability over perfection. Read this book deliberately, in order, and as a system being built piece by piece.

The Growth Gap Toolkit

Everything you need to implement the system in this book is available in one place. The toolkit includes the Growth Gap Scorecard, example P&L, CEO First 30 Day Checklist, and more.

Visit toolkit.ecommercegrowthgap.com to access all resources.

Reader's Guide: Everything you need to close your Ecommerce Growth Gap - Scan to access guides, templates & tool - all in one place

PREFACE

I've spent over twenty years building and leading eCommerce businesses within branded consumer products companies. I've had responsibility for revenue, contribution margin, budgets, forecasting, and ultimately, the accountability associated with each of these areas. In addition to driving growth, I've been accountable for ensuring it was profitable, predictable, and sustainable.

Across those years, I've seen a consistent theme emerge, regardless of the company or industry I'm working with or in. Digital teams are extremely busy, there's an abundance of data being analyzed through an array of dashboards, projects are always underway, and everyone is working incredibly hard. Despite all the activity and passion, profitability has often eroded, and the true potential of eCommerce remains unrealized.

That disconnect is what I refer to as the *eCommerce Growth Gap*: the tangible difference between the potential of a brand's digital channels and the brand's actual financial performance. Once you're able to identify the gap, it's virtually impossible to ignore. The Growth Gap explains why so many eCommerce teams are constantly under pressure and have little evidence of meaningful progress, why CEOs find themselves unable to determine what is truly effective and what isn't, and why board members are increasingly losing confidence in their investment in digital platforms that fail to generate the returns on which they based their decisions.

The Growth Gap is not due to a lack of enthusiasm, energy, or tools. It exists because most companies do not have a clear understanding of how eCommerce operates as a business system. As such, most organizations treat eCommerce as nothing more than a collection of channels instead of a single commercial engine. They respond to symptoms rather than diagnosing the root causes of issues. They make business decisions based on incomplete and inaccurate information related to their eCommerce activities. And they operate without the cross-functional alignment required to turn digital activity into durable profit.

eCommerce is not a mystery. Fundamentally, it's a commercial system, and many brands have failed to manage it effectively simply because they lacked the required knowledge and understanding.

As I reflect on the past two decades, I have come to realize that the knowledge required to close the Growth Gap exists, but it is scattered across the eCommerce industry. High-performing teams share a mental model—a way of thinking about eCommerce as a system, interpreting relevant signals, making sequential decisions, and maximizing profit. Unfortunately, this shared mental model exists primarily as tribal knowledge within a small number of teams and is therefore not typically documented or shared with other organizations where it could be applied.

This book is my attempt to change that. It is the book I wish I could have read when I was given my first P&L and asked to "make eCommerce succeed." It summarizes everything I have learned from building teams, turning around underperforming eCommerce businesses, and working closely with executives who genuinely care about delivering real results.

Your brand is not unique in its challenges, and the eCommerce Growth Gap is solvable. This book will teach you how to close the gap, achieve your goals, and unlock profitable growth.

INTRODUCTION

The Real Problem Behind eCommerce Underperformance

"I just read that our main competitor reports that 50 percent of their revenue comes from eCommerce. My business is only at 10 percent. The board is pressuring me about it. My team can't provide an answer or plan that makes sense. We've been spending money but just staying afloat. What in the world are we doing wrong?"

This question from a CEO, or some form of it, has been the starting point of more conversations throughout my career than I can count.

Most brands assume they have an eCommerce marketing or technology problem. In my experience, that's rarely the full story. They have a system problem, but their leaders can't see it clearly. After all, it's hard to read the label from inside the bottle.

Each day, brands experience the symptoms of this problem. Growth has slowed down despite an increase in spending. The cost of acquiring customers is increasing. The lifetime value of customers is decreasing. Margins are being compressed. Forecasts are becoming unreliable. Employees are busy, yet they are slow in executing the plan and making progress. The number of meetings is increasing, but decision-making is decelerating. Confidence within the C-suite and boardroom is decreasing.

We've all heard the common reasons for these problems: "The market is soft." "Ad costs are up." "Creative assets need improvement." "The agency isn't delivering." "The team needs more resources." Those explanations are incomplete at best and flat-out wrong at worst. The real issue is systemic and structural.

Most eCommerce businesses operate without a unified system. Strategy, economics, marketing, merchandising, operations, finance, and technology are operating as separate components rather than working together to produce a cohesive outcome. Decisions get made in isolation, the trade-offs associated with each decision remain invisible, and accountability becomes blurred. This leads to a reactive and volatile business.

This is the Growth Gap in action. Each misaligned decision contributes to the drift away from optimal performance. Each unclear priority adds additional friction to the process. Every tactical fix pushes the real problem further out of sight.

System problems don't respond to tactical fixes. Increasing the marketing spend does not restore strategic clarity. Adding additional tools won't create alignment. Creating more dashboards will not improve decision-making. Hiring more people will not fix broken economics. eCommerce is not simply a digital channel; it is a business system that includes structure, sequencing, interdependencies, and specific financial logic. Brands that understand this build momentum. Brands that don't burn time, money, and talent while wondering why progress feels so hard.

This book is designed to accomplish three things.

First, it clarifies the real causes of underperformance. These are not the symptoms you see in dashboards and hear discussed in meeting rooms but the structural issues that accumulate over time, often going unnoticed.

Second, it explains the structure of a healthy eCommerce business as an intentional system that aligns strategy, economics, demand generation, operations, and customer experience around shared outcomes.

Third, it provides a practical blueprint for closing the Growth Gap, using frameworks, diagnostics, and operating principles that leaders can apply both immediately and as a longer-term road map.

This is an operator's book. It was written with the same approach high-performing eCommerce teams bring to work each day: less noise, more outcomes. It prioritizes frameworks, diagnostics, and operating shifts you can apply immediately rather than long anecdotes and filler.

The following pages are not a collection of tactics or quick fixes. Instead, they offer a clear view of how successful eCommerce businesses operate beneath the surface and explain why most brands struggle to build systems that scale profitably.

If your brand's eCommerce business is growing more slowly than it should, spending more money to achieve less, or struggling to turn activity into results, the causes are not mysterious. Once the system becomes visible, the actual problems become clear. And once the exact issues are clear, you can finally close the Growth Gap.

So let's begin where the real problems live.

A MAP FOR THE JOURNEY AHEAD

The eCommerce Value-Creation System

This book is built around a single organizing model.

Every diagnosis in Part 1, every root cause in Part 2, and every solution in Part 3 connects back to the framework on the following page: the **eCommerce Value-Creation System**. Before you begin, it is worth pausing to review, because this diagram is not just an illustration. It is the architecture of a high-performance eCommerce business.

The system is structured like a building, and it behaves like one. At the base sits the eCommerce Value Chain. This is the operating rhythm that connects strategy to execution, execution to insight, and insight to better decisions. Without it, nothing above holds.

Rising from that foundation are four pillars: the strategic and financial logic that governs the business, the demand engine that drives growth, the capabilities and ownership structures that enable execution, and the infrastructure and operations that make speed possible. These pillars do not operate independently. Weaken one and the system strains. Remove one and performance collapses.

Across the top of those pillars rest two beams, profitable growth and operational excellence, which represent the dual outcomes a healthy eCommerce business produces simultaneously.

And at the apex sits eCommerce Value Creation: the point at which growth, margin, brand strength, customer lifetime value, and organizational confidence reinforce one another. This is where the Growth Gap closes for good.

Part 1 of this book will show you where this system breaks down and why. Part 2 will name the five forces responsible for those breakdowns. Part 3 will show you how to build, govern, and run the system so that it compounds performance over time.

Keep this diagram close. Every chapter adds a layer to it.

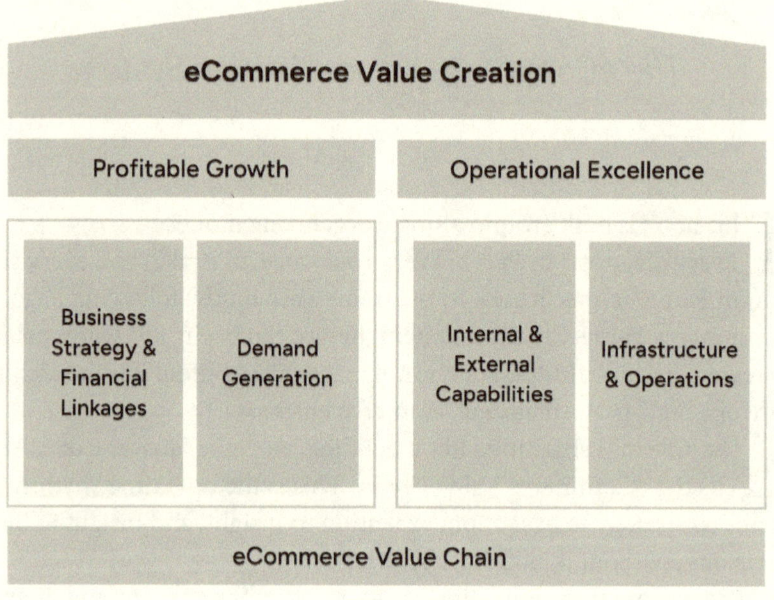

PART 1

THE GROWTH GAP

When Performance Lags Potential

CHAPTER 1

The eCommerce Growth Gap

Where Effort Increases but Outcomes Erode

How do we declare success in eCommerce? Revenue growth? Profitability? Gross margins? Traffic? Conversion rate? Benchmarks? Long-range plans? All of the above?

As with assessing talent within your organization, measuring success in an eCommerce business is not binary. However, throughout my career, the eCommerce businesses that were "failing" all shared a common trait: The organization knew eCommerce performance did not match its potential. Perhaps eCommerce penetration wasn't high enough, or revenue growth didn't match competitors, or profitability was eroding every year.

Just like when you have an underperforming employee on your team, when performance doesn't match potential, feedback and corrective action are required to close the gap.

Most organizations misdiagnose the problem, attributing it to ad spend, agencies, attribution models, platforms, creative talent, the economy, or insufficient budgets.

These issues may be real, but they represent symptoms, not the cause.

The Growth Gap arises when digital activity outpaces a company's clarity, capability, and financial acumen. It is what happens when a complex, high-stakes business is operated without a shared blueprint. Until leadership can see the system clearly, the gap widens.

How the Growth Gap Reveals Itself

The pattern is consistent across midmarket brands:

- Efforts to generate growth increase, but growth rates decrease.
- Customer acquisition costs (CAC) increase without an apparent explanation.
- Retention rates and customer lifetime value (LTV) plateau or decline.
- Discounting becomes habitual.
- Reporting grows noisier while decision-making becomes more difficult.
- Meetings multiply as confidence decreases.

Leadership is frustrated, the board of directors is frustrated, and employees are frustrated. Everyone senses the strain but cannot get aligned.

This is the Growth Gap in full force: a brand that has a great deal of growth potential but is achieving subpar financial results while putting in more effort than ever before.

Why the Gap Exists

Five Forces create the Growth Gap, each of which is discussed next.

1. Inadequate Strategy

More often than not, brands do not clearly define the role of eCommerce in their overall business strategy. Thus, the marketing department strives to maximize growth. Financial departments strive to maximize margins. Merchandising departments strive to maximize sell-through. Operations departments strive to optimize predictability. Without a clear, shared model, eCommerce is typically managed reactively rather than strategically.

2. Financial Blind Spots

Brands often misunderstand or ignore contribution margin, variable profit, cost-to-serve, and channel profitability. Return on ad spend (ROAS) is used as a proxy for financial acumen. The number of reports and dashboards continues to grow, but decision-making is increasingly removed from the business's economics.

3. Capability Gaps

eCommerce requires cross-functional operators who understand acquisition, merchandising, user experience (UX), retention, and the profit and loss statement (P&L) simultaneously. Most organizations are built on wholesale DNA (more on this to come). Ownership is diluted. Authority is unclear. Even strong teams struggle without structural clarity.

4. Infrastructure and Process Debt

Tools are purchased much faster than processes are developed. Decision authority is ambiguous. Planning becomes inconsistent and priorities change weekly. What should function as a system degrades into disconnected activities.

5. Demand Misalignment

Acquisition, retention, creative, conversion-rate optimization, and merchandising operate independently. Budgets are not linked to contribution margin. CAC rises faster than LTV. Discounts compensate for a weak demand engine, training customers to wait for promotions.

Each force adds noise and contributes to confusion, which in turn reduces leadership confidence. Once leadership loses confidence, the Growth Gap accelerates.

Why Most Fixes Fail

When a brand's performance stagnates, most organizations increase activity to drive higher performance. They add new channels, creative assets, tools, meetings, reports, and tactics.

Increasing activity levels does nothing but worsen the problem.

Activity without disciplined and systemic alignment generates noise, noise without leadership creates drift, and drift without financial discipline produces bad decisions. The organization is now expending twice the effort and achieving significantly lower returns.

The Growth Gap cannot be closed through increased activity. It closes through clarity, systems, and disciplined leadership.

The Growth Gap Is Fixable

The Growth Gap is neither random nor permanent. Once the system is observable, the way forward will become clear and definable, and leaders will find that the team can make progress at a much faster rate than anticipated.

eCommerce is not a mystery. It is a system. If that system is operated cohesively, it can be one of the best strategic growth engines that a brand can develop. If not, it can be one of the most costly.

Before developing solutions to address the system, leaders need to identify where it is failing.

CEO BRIEFING

- **Truth:** The Growth Gap originates from broken systems. No amount of tweaking marketing spend will correct a structural misalignment.
- **Red Flag:** If your team is hitting marketing targets like ROAS while cash flow or contribution margin remain flat, the Growth Gap is widening.
- **Key Question:** "Do we have a shared, documented financial definition of the eCommerce contribution margin that both the marketing and finance departments have signed off on?"

OPERATOR DIAGNOSTIC

Answer **Yes** or **No** to each question.

1. Do you have a clear, unified definition of what eCommerce is supposed to achieve?
2. Are the marketing, finance, operations, and merchandising departments aligned on shared goals and decision criteria?
3. Do you understand the true contribution margin of each channel?

4. Are decisions driven by economics rather than dashboards or vanity metrics?
5. Is your organizational structure designed for how eCommerce actually works?
6. Are acquisition, retention, creative, customer experience (CX), and merchandising managed as one system?
7. Do you operate on a clear, predictable planning and decision cadence?
8. Is your tech stack enabling speed, not slowing it down?
9. Can leadership clearly explain why performance changed in the past year?
10. Does the organization have a coherent blueprint for profitable eCommerce growth?

Scoring and Interpretation

Yes to 8–10 questions: Your Growth Gap is narrow and solvable with focus.

Yes to 5–7 questions: Your Growth Gap is moderate. Fundamentals exist but are disconnected.

Yes to 0–4 questions: Your Growth Gap is structural. Performance will not improve without addressing the system.

Summary

The eCommerce Growth Gap is the predictable outcome of running a complex retail business without the strategy, economics, operating model, and infrastructure required to scale. When the system is misaligned, effort increases, but performance lags, and the organization loses confidence in the channel.

Closing the Growth Gap starts by naming it clearly and recognizing it as a system failure that spans the entire operation, rather than a collection of isolated issues.

Next, we define how the Growth Gap routinely shows up inside brands and how to recognize the symptoms before the business starts blaming the wrong causes.

The Growth Gap Fatal Twenty Executive Diagnostic

Answer each question **Yes** or **No**. Do not overthink the answers. Hint: If the answer requires explanation, it is likely a "No."

Strategy and Role Clarity

1. Can you clearly articulate the primary role eCommerce plays in your business today: growth engine, profit center, or brand builder?
2. Is that role documented and consistently used to guide decisions across marketing, finance, product, and operations?
3. Have you explicitly decided which metrics matter most and which trade-offs are already settled?
4. If asked, could your leadership team independently describe the same eCommerce strategy without contradiction?

Financial Truth and Economics

5. Do you have a single, agreed-upon definition of the eCommerce contribution margin, represented in a monthly P&L, that the marketing and finance departments both trust?
6. Can you state your allowable CAC based on customer LTV, not ROAS targets?
7. Do you know which products, customer segments, or channels create value and which destroy it?
8. When performance changes, can your team explain *why* in economic terms, not just channel metrics?

Ownership and Accountability

9. Is there one clearly accountable owner for end-to-end eCommerce performance, including the top-to-bottom P&L?
10. Does that owner have real authority or influence over the inputs that drive results, not just responsibility for the outcome?
11. Are decision rights clear enough that most decisions do not require escalation, consensus, or design by committee?
12. When performance misses, does the team bring diagnoses and plans rather than explanations and excuses?

Operating Discipline and Cadence

13. Do you have a protected and high-stakes weekly forum that produces decisions and actions, not just reporting?
14. Are monthly reviews used to identify patterns and adjust the system rather than react to noise?
15. Does your annual plan reconcile top-down ambition with bottom-up reality before execution begins?
16. Are priorities stable enough that teams can execute without renegotiating direction every week?

Demand and Growth Quality

17. Is demand being earned and compounded through brand and retention, or is it primarily rented through paid media spend?
18. Is customer LTV increasing year over year, not just traffic or revenue?
19. If paid spend were reduced tomorrow, would demand meaningfully persist?
20. Do you trust your eCommerce team to deliver its forecast?

Scoring and Interpretation

Yes to 16–20 questions: Your Growth Gap is narrow. Performance issues are likely isolated and solvable with focus and discipline.

Yes to 11–15 questions: Your Growth Gap is real. The system functions in places, but misalignment is setting a ceiling on performance.

Yes to 6–10 questions: Your Growth Gap is structural. Effort is high, clarity is low, and growth will remain fragile.

Yes to 0–5 questions: You do not have an eCommerce growth system. You have activity, talent, and spending without a governing model.

Executive Warning

If you scored below 12, *more activity will not fix this.*
More spending, more tools, or more meetings will widen the gap.
That is what this book is designed to resolve.

CHAPTER 2

Growth Gap Symptoms

How Structural Misalignment Hides in Plain Sight

Do you have a Growth Gap? In my experience, the Growth Gap does not knock on the door and announce itself directly. It doesn't show up in board meetings, one-on-ones, or business reviews wearing a name badge.

Instead, it presents itself through patterns that may appear unrelated but all point to the same truth. Your eCommerce business has become misaligned. Your activity, KPIs, and financial performance are no longer reinforcing one another or making logical sense together.

Brands often misinterpret these signs. They commonly attribute their lack of success to their employees, agencies, or the marketplace. Even more alarming, some wind up declaring, "eCommerce does not fit for my brand."

Misinterpreting symptoms is dangerous. The symptoms do not accurately reflect the underlying problem. Symptoms are just evidence that the system is no longer functioning correctly.

Financial Symptoms: When the Numbers Stop Making Sense

Financial signals usually appear first because the economics break down before organizations understand why.

Your CAC is rising, ROAS decreases, and your contribution margins narrow. Your LTV stops growing. Average order values decline, you start discounting to backfill revenue shortfalls, and your forecasts become less stable.

Many executives view these changes as isolated marketing issues: "The media mix is incorrect." "The creative assets need to be improved." "The agency is underperforming."

However, financial symptoms rarely belong to a single channel or tactic. Financial symptoms reflect a systemic failure to generate and capture value. When activity no longer translates into KPIs, and KPIs no longer translate into profitable growth, something is structurally wrong.

Operational Symptoms: Doing More With Fewer Results

As performance softens, operations begin to strain.

Discipline is lost in planning and priorities are shifted midcycle. Deadlines are pushed back and decision-making slows down. Reporting increases as a form of defensive posturing. When teams cannot produce results, they produce data instead. When your weekly dashboard report is growing larger than normal, yet your revenue remains stagnant, you're observing the system attempting to conceal its own failure.

Meetings multiply. The team works harder, yet the correlation between effort and success continues to decline.

One clear and common red flag is when no team member can provide a confident explanation of what occurred during the previous week or month. The data exist, but there is no shared framework to interpret the data. Absent a system, activity and data become noise, which widens the Growth Gap.

Organizational Symptoms: Loss of Confidence

Internally, a consistent tension emerges as a result of the Growth Gap.

The C-suite expects more growth. The eCommerce team believes it is at maximum capacity. Finance wants more margin, Marketing wants more money for campaigns, and Merchandising wants better sell-through. Ownership and roles become ambiguous. Meetings transition from decision-making to swirling debates. Leadership and the board lose confidence in the plan, and the team loses confidence in leadership.

This loss of confidence is typically attributed to a lack of talent or effort. However, this symptom represents a system that no longer provides adequate strategic direction or executional alignment.

Customer and Market Symptoms: The Brand Loses Momentum

While the team is struggling internally, customer feedback also signals the problems.

Repeat customers are no longer repeating. Returns are rising. The website's performance is becoming inconsistent and customers are buying fewer items or trading down. While traffic is growing, revenue is not. Competitors are starting to gain market share with similar levels of resources.

These symptoms are often attributed to the marketplace or changing consumer behavior. More often than not, these signals indicate internal friction, including slow testing cycles, inconsistent product stories, poor retention design, and friction in the customer journey.

When multiple customer, financial, operational, and organizational symptoms are present together, the Growth Gap has crossed from emerging to fully established.

Why Symptoms Are Misleading

Symptoms are observable but untrustworthy because they do not point to the actual source of the problem and thus drive us to take the wrong corrective actions.

Regardless, most organizations react to symptoms, usually by increasing activity. Budgets are adjusted on a weekly basis. Additional tools are purchased. Agencies are expanded. The pressure mounts, but the desired outcomes remain absent.

A typical follow-on response is to reduce eCommerce spending and focus on wholesale because wholesale seems easier to predict. This is the opposite of the correct conclusion. The eCommerce channel is not the problem. The operating model used to run the channel is.

Adding more activity will not close the gap. Producing more reports will not close the gap. Adding a platform or tool will not close the gap.

Closing the gap requires system-level rewiring.

The Turning Point

Once leadership understands symptoms correctly, the environment rapidly changes.

Confusion gives way to clarity, and debate gives way to alignment. Teams stop arguing over data interpretation and start identifying the fundamental constraints.

The company acknowledges that the model, not the channel, is failing, and the model can be fixed.

Symptoms no longer feel like noise but instead serve as a diagnostic map showing how far the system has drifted and where to begin realigning it.

Attempting to address symptoms is similar to playing Whac-A-Mole. To eliminate the noise, you need to move upstream to the underlying structural failures that are causing it.

CEO BRIEFING

- **Truth:** Symptoms are not the problem. They are evidence that the system connecting activity, KPIs, and economics is broken.
- **Red Flag:** If multiple teams are optimizing their own metrics while overall performance keeps slipping, the system is misaligned.
- **Key Question:** "Can we clearly explain why performance changed last month, and do all teams agree on the explanation?"

OPERATOR DIAGNOSTIC

Answer **Yes** or **No** to each question.

1. Are your financial indicators trending in the wrong direction?
2. Does your team feel busier while results remain flat?
3. Do planning cycles frequently shift or break down?
4. Do cross-functional teams disagree on priorities?
5. Is there tension between leadership and the eCommerce team?
6. Are dashboards multiplying without improving clarity?
7. Are discounts becoming a larger part of your revenue mix?
8. Is retention stagnating or declining?
9. Are competitors beginning to outpace you?

10. Are there conflicting narratives about why performance changed last month?

Scoring and Interpretation

Yes to 8–10 questions: Symptoms are widespread and require structural correction.

Yes to 5–7 questions: Symptoms are moderate and reflect misalignment.

Yes to 0–4 questions: Symptoms are emerging and can be addressed early.

Summary

Growth Gap symptoms are the visible signals of deeper structural failure. These symptoms are often treated as separate problems, but they are connected signs of the same underlying systemic issues.

When leadership reacts to symptoms instead of diagnosing root causes, the Growth Gap widens even when execution appears disciplined.

Next, we dismantle the most common misconception in eCommerce: that growth is simply a matter of spending more, working harder, and finding better tactics.

CHAPTER 3

The Myth of "Just Spend and Do More"

Why Activity Cannot Fix Broken Economics

"We're not doing enough. I want to see the list of actions!"

This is a common CEO reaction to their team's weekly or monthly business report when eCommerce is experiencing a Growth Gap. The illusion of control creeps in, and everyone gets uncomfortable unless there is a long list of actions every week. But busyness is not effectiveness.

When eCommerce growth stalls, nearly all brands reach for the same solution: Spend and do more.

It seems logical. With increased advertising spend, traffic will increase, and with more traffic, sales will rise. And in theory, spending money should turn the tap on to generate more growth. It feels like an investment that will produce a return.

That logic is often wrong or, at best, incomplete. And brands find out the hard way that spending more money on advertising does not improve weak economics. In fact, it can make the economics worse. "Spend more" is not a strategy or solution.

Why "Just Spend More" Fails

When an eCommerce business experiences softer-than-expected performance (e.g., rising CACs, stagnant sales), the first response of nearly all businesses is that their marketing needs to be addressed: "We need to review and analyze the channels, creative assets, and agencies involved!"

However, the problem lies with the assumption that volume is the limiting factor (i.e., increasing ad spend). It usually isn't. For example, if a brand has poor retention rates, then acquiring new customers will be inefficient. If a brand has thin margins, then spending cannot be scaled. If the incentives are misaligned or if no one owns the process, then execution will be inconsistent. When these fundamentals are off, more budget only accelerates poor performance.

The belief that "spend equals growth" indicates that the business treats marketing as the primary growth driver rather than recognizing that the operating model beneath the business is what either enables or constrains growth.

You've likely encountered these businesses. They are growing top-line revenue at an impressive clip while profit drags, perhaps even unknowingly. A dollar goes out in marketing for a dollar to come in as revenue. We call this a "red-hot money loser." They always have a short lifespan.

The Conversations Leaders Avoid

Tactically focused discussions allow organizations to avoid discussing more complex and potentially challenging topics.

For instance, the discussion may focus on reviewing channels or analyzing campaign results, with weekly fluctuations in ROAS often at the center of each week's discussion.

Meanwhile, retention issues, poor unit economics, and low contribution margins are either ignored or poorly understood. Additionally, organizational misalignment is rarely discussed because it is perceived as much more complicated to fix than changing agencies or rolling out new campaigns.

Leadership conversations and marketing conversations are two different things. The former requires alignment across multiple functions and rigorous analysis of financial metrics. Unfortunately, many organizations avoid these discussions because they believe new tactics are more actionable, even when they don't deliver meaningful change in outcomes.

As a result, the outcome is easy to predict. Symptoms are treated while the causes remain unaddressed, and the Growth Gap continues to get worse.

The Tactical Fixes That Don't Work

When a brand is feeling stuck, there are typically three common responses:

1. Changing agencies.
2. Rebuilding the website.
3. Chasing shiny objects.

Changing Agencies

A new agency always brings new ideas, new people, and new creative assets. However, if the underlying economics of your business are broken or unclear, every agency will struggle.

Rebuilding the Website

New user experiences, new content management systems, and new platforms can bring excitement and optimism. Unfortunately, without addressing pricing, assortment, contribution margin, and underlying operational friction, the outcome will be the same.

Chasing Shiny Objects

New channels, tools, and attribution methods can create significant changes but little actual progress. The complexity of the business increases while the results do not.

All of these responses fail for the same reason: They do not address the underlying system. They merely add additional activity to a broken system.

The Breakthrough Insight

There is one insight that has a profound impact on the way organizations approach their challenges: Contribution margin is the engine of profitable growth.

Until you have sufficient profit per order, you cannot reasonably expect to scale your spending sustainably. Any increase in spending will only exacerbate existing weaknesses in your business.

When organizations realize this, priorities shift. Rather than debating which channel is best, they begin debating which economics are most important. Organizations also start to focus on the mechanics of retaining customers, merchandising effectively, pricing correctly, optimizing the performance of the website, and streamlining operations in order to drive greater efficiencies through the customer acquisition process. Marketing is no longer treated as a separate entity from the rest of the business and instead is integrated into the overall system.

From that point forward, "just spend and do more" loses its luster. That approach reveals itself as an accelerator of whatever system already exists.

The Leadership Shift

This chapter is not advocating for less spending. It advocates discipline and effectiveness.

To achieve sustainable growth, leaders must move beyond tactical reflexes and confront the structural limitations of their business. This means transitioning from discussing specific channels to making decisions about the entire system.

When that shift takes place, clarity supplants confusion. Teams begin to operate based on contribution margin rather than individual KPIs and decision-making becomes better. Predictable outcomes become achievable.

At that point, responsibility supplants noise. The organization recognizes that the symptoms were just masking underlying system problems, and the team must now work to address them.

CEO BRIEFING

- **Truth:** You cannot buy your way out of weak economics. More spending amplifies the system you already have.
- **Red Flag:** If increasing the budget produces more activity but not more profit, the constraint is structural.
- **Key Question:** "What is our true contribution margin per order, and does it support scaled acquisition?"

OPERATOR DIAGNOSTIC

Answer **Yes** or **No** to each question.

1. Do you increase spending when growth slows, hoping it will recover performance?
2. Does your team debate channels and campaigns more than economics and retention?
3. Have you changed agencies more than once in the last three years?
4. Have you rebuilt or redesigned your website multiple times to solve conversion issues?
5. Do new tools or channels regularly get introduced to "fix" performance?
6. Do you treat ROAS as the primary indicator of marketing health?
7. Is the contribution margin unclear or rarely discussed?
8. Are retention and customer value secondary topics compared with acquisition?
9. Do cross-functional teams disagree on why performance is inconsistent?
10. Does leadership have limited confidence in why increasing spending does or doesn't work?

Scoring and Interpretation

Yes to 8–10 questions: You are treating symptoms, not causes.

Yes to 5–7 questions: Your model needs clarification and alignment.

Yes to 0–4 questions: Tactical drift is emerging and should be corrected early.

Summary

The "just spend and do more" myth is the fastest way to deepen the Growth Gap. Brands attempt to outwork structural problems with activity, but activity cannot fix broken economics, unclear strategy, weak governance, or operational constraints. Over time, growth becomes more expensive, more volatile, and more dependent on promotions and short-term wins.

The Growth Gap closes when leadership stops optimizing activity and starts governing the system that produces outcomes.

Next, we more thoroughly define eCommerce as a business system with interconnected levers, where success depends on alignment across functions, not isolated channel performance.

CHAPTER 4

eCommerce as a System

From Disconnected Functions to a Unified Growth Engine

Does your eCommerce business sometimes feel like it would make Rube Goldberg blush? Lots of complexity, lots of moving parts doing things they weren't designed to do, and an underwhelming output?

When eCommerce is treated as a collection of parts, each component is optimized independently. Performance marketing has its goals, the site has its road map, the retention team has its strategy, the brand department has its own objectives, and operations and merchandising have their own rhythms. Each component is evaluated independently by leadership, and the entire engine cannot be measured as a cohesive unit.

Optimizing eCommerce in isolation will never produce sustainable results. While the components may perform well individually, they must operate interdependently to achieve sustainable performance.

When all components of eCommerce (acquisition, conversion, retention, economics, etc.) reinforce one another, eCommerce performance reaches its full potential. When they do not, the effort required to achieve desired results increases, and performance declines.

Interdependence in eCommerce

Most brands and eCommerce teams would not disagree that acquisition, conversion, and retention are related. However, they also tend to believe they can scale each component independently.

Acquisition efficiency depends on high-quality merchandise, compelling storytelling, a functional eCommerce site, and transactional economics. Conversion depends on price, assortment, availability, content, trust, and user experience. Retention depends on the customer's experience with products, delivery and fulfillment, customer service, and lifecycle communications.

And still, brands commonly treat these components separately. When one component underperforms, another typically compensates. However, over time, inefficiencies in the system will become apparent, and progress overall will be lost.

Where Brands Overfocus and Underinvest

eCommerce teams tend to focus too heavily on performance marketing and the website.

Creative assets, audiences, attribution, funnels, and user experience receive extensive amounts of resources and focus. Lower-funnel performance-based paid media receives an excessive share of the budget because it is perceived as a controllable, immediately impactful channel. Additionally, sites are continuously rebuilt with the expectation that the design or platform is the constraint.

Conversely, organizations often invest insufficiently in retention, storytelling, strategy, and channel alignment. Organizations assume that lifecycle marketing will address retention issues on its own.

In addition, brands typically do not understand customer value well enough. They generally view storytelling as a campaign asset rather than a conversion driver. Finally, brands often face channel conflict due to the internal political difficulty of resolving conflicting incentives.

Overinvesting in one component, such as paid media, at the expense of others, such as retention, will create diminishing returns. Acquisition costs increase, conversion plateaus, and retention weakens.

To compensate for the loss of performance, marketing spending continues to increase, which negatively affects the economics. As a result, paid media becomes a pressure valve rather than a system input.

How the Real Constraint Becomes Obvious

When leaders evaluate their eCommerce business systemically for the first time, the constraints usually become obvious.

Typically, the core constraint does not turn out to be the campaigns, the website, or the agency.

In the majority of cases, the structural constraint exists in one of two areas:

1. Strategy and Financial Linkages: The business does not have a clear understanding of the eCommerce strategic role, the contribution margin required to scale, or the economic guardrails that guide investment decisions. Therefore, the system cannot operate with precision.
2. Internal Capability: Ownership is unclear. Roles are misaligned. Teams are either overextended or working at cross-purposes. Even strong talent struggles when the operating model is not designed for success.

This is not a functional problem. It's a business unit problem.

What a Healthy System Feels Like

When a healthy eCommerce system is in place, the way people behave inside an organization changes.

Leaders can trust the data provided by the system because it produces consistent, easy-to-understand information. Teams have a clear understanding of "good" performance across the entire engine, not just within their individual function. Meetings are shorter, decisions are quicker, and people feel less stressed executing the plans.

Even if performance falls short of expectations at first, the plan still makes sense. Leaders know the reasoning behind the plan, the timing, and the trade-offs. They remain confident in the team's ability to execute the plan because the system provides the necessary context.

Healthy systems don't eliminate problems, but they absolutely make problems easier to identify and solve.

Why Systems Outperform Tactics

Tactics can create short-term movement, but systems build long-term value. Systems remove friction, provide predictability, create aligned incentives, and compound learning.

When eCommerce is managed as a single, holistic business unit, all functions work toward the same objective. Acquisition enables conversion. Conversion enables retention. Retention enables stronger contribution margins. Contribution margins determine how much acquisition can grow. Operations can now deliver on the brand's promises. Storytelling reinforces customer value throughout the journey.

The result is not a reduction in activity but *better* activity, aligned toward measurable outcomes.

The Operating Mindset

Closing the Growth Gap requires a fundamental shift in how eCommerce leaders view their businesses.

They must shift from thinking of eCommerce as a marketing channel, online store, or collection of unrelated functions to seeing it as a business unit complete with its own strategy, economics, operating model, and cross-functional dependencies.

When eCommerce leaders begin viewing their business as a true business unit, their growth constraints will become apparent. Then, priorities will become clearer, decision-making will improve, and the growth engine will stabilize.

CEO BRIEFING

- **Truth:** eCommerce performance breaks when functions are optimized independently instead of managed as a unified business system.
- **Red Flag:** If teams are hitting their individual KPIs while overall performance remains inconsistent, the system is fragmented.
- **Key Question:** "Who owns eCommerce end to end, and do they have authority across marketing, merchandising, operations, and economics?"

OPERATOR DIAGNOSTIC

Answer **Yes** or **No** to each question.

1. Do acquisition, conversion, and retention operate as one engine?
2. Does every team understand its role in the system?
3. Are contribution margin and economic guardrails clearly defined?
4. Does eCommerce have cross-functional clarity and ownership?
5. Are retention and storytelling treated as core drivers of growth?
6. Are channel conflicts resolved through strategy rather than politics?
7. Does leadership trust the numbers produced by the system?
8. Are plans based on economics rather than tactics?
9. Do teams move quickly because priorities are clear?
10. Does eCommerce operate as a holistic business unit rather than a collection of parts?

Scoring and Interpretation

Yes to 8–10 questions: The system is functioning as a unified engine.

Yes to 5–7 questions: The system is partially aligned but requires strengthening.

Yes to 0–4 questions: The system is fragmented and limiting growth.

Summary

eCommerce is not simply a digital marketing channel. It is a retail business unit made of interconnected systems: strategy, economics, demand, conversion, retention, operations, and infrastructure. When those systems are fragmented, the organization debates tactics, misreads signals, and struggles to scale profitably. When those systems are aligned, growth becomes more predictable, durable, and financially grounded.

The Growth Gap is fundamentally a systems problem, which means it can only be solved with systems thinking and systems leadership.

Next, we address the hardest truth in the Growth Gap: The gap persists primarily because leadership behavior, ownership, and decision discipline are not designed for eCommerce.

CHAPTER 5

The Growth Gap Is Mostly a Leadership Problem

Clarity, Discipline, and the Cost of Strategic Avoidance

One uncomfortable truth consistently rears its head in brands that get stuck in a perpetual Growth Gap. They have a leadership problem.

When leaders lack clarity and discipline, the rest of the team loses confidence. When teams lose confidence, their execution becomes reactive. When execution is reactive, you get an environment filled with noise. In environments where noise prevails, regardless of how much you spend on tools or head count, you will never achieve sustainable, predictable profit.

Leaders need to have the courage to accurately identify the underlying cause beneath the dashboards, tactics, and debates—the one few organizations are willing to confront.

Leaders set the climate and context for your eCommerce performance. Everything else—strategy, expectations, alignment, and financial understanding—flows down from there.

The Real Constraint

These lapses are always understandable. Leaders are inundated with various metrics, opinions, and recommendations for tactical adjustments. Agencies promote optimization opportunities, vendors tout new tools, teams submit logical requests, and industry trends seem to change weekly. Everyone has a slide, a smoking gun, and urgency.

Signal disappears, direction gets fuzzy, and execution disintegrates.

Because eCommerce is a complex system, maintaining clarity is essential. When leadership loses clarity, it breaks the connective tissue linking acquisition, conversion, and retention in your system. Your business then transitions from being managed as an integrated whole to being managed as individual workstreams.

In such an environment, even very strong teams will underperform. Even healthy budgets are squandered. Even reasonable strategies will not build momentum.

Leadership Clarity Trumps Marketing Talent

Talented teams can outperform their peers in execution. However, even gifted teams cannot truly overcome a broken system.

Three leadership responsibilities consistently determine whether a brand can close the Growth Gap.

First: Trust the Numbers

Your eCommerce business becomes impossible to manage when nobody believes the data. Marketing believes the platform's ROAS data. Finance trusts none of it. Analytics creates multiple different models to support alternative realities. Everyone defends their own version of reality.

Politics inevitably enters decision-making.

All high-performing eCommerce organizations rely on a single financial model based on the contribution margin to make investment decisions. These organizations understand their P&L like the back of their hand. They know how average order value (AOV), conversion rate (CVR), repeat rate, and cost-to-serve work together. All investment decisions are made based on economic principles, not simply dashboard metrics.

When leaders believe the numbers, the teams become aligned. If they don't, the teams begin to fight instead.

Second: Define What "Good" Looks Like

When expectations are ambiguous, teams tend to wander. When "good" is defined ambiguously, success becomes retrospective, and failure is personal. Accountability ultimately disappears.

Disciplined organizations remove ambiguity by defining targets before they are achieved. They align KPIs to financial results. Expectations are specific and shared.

When "good" is defined clearly, performance improves.

Third: Respond Instead of React

Volatility is inevitable. Markets change; algorithms change. Targets are missed.

Disciplined organizations respond rather than react.

Reaction is when thinking is replaced with urgency. Budgets get cut, agencies get replaced, websites get rebuilt, and new tools are added.

Responding is when organizations diagnose first and act second. They identify the root cause, the constraint, and the plan to regain performance. With the whole system front and center, the team can provide answers and a logical path forward.

The difference is not talent. The difference is clarity.

Factors That Cause Leadership Discipline to Erode

Discipline is lost as a result of common and consistent factors across struggling brands:

- Too many metrics and too little insight ("data rich, insight poor")
- Shiny objects and smoking guns that promise shortcuts
- Tactical debates detached from economics
- Industry hype that ignores unit economics
- Internal politics and misaligned incentives

As these factors continue to accumulate, leadership shifts from directing a system to refereeing noise, and the Growth Gap continues to grow.

Characteristics of Disciplined Teams

Disciplined teams have common characteristics:

- When leadership clarity is high, behaviors change rapidly.
- There is one truth. Conflicts center on direction, not data.
- Everyone understands what "good" is. Targets are defined and understood.
- If performance misses expectations, the team can define the diagnosis, the plan, and the trade-offs.
- Leadership provides direction and support for executing the plan.
- Confidence supplants chaos, and progress replaces panic.
- The organization becomes capable of closing the Growth Gap.

We will revisit leadership and actionable steps to ensure a disciplined eCommerce business multiple times in the remaining chapters.

CEO BRIEFING

- **Truth:** eCommerce performance degrades when leadership allows noise to replace clarity.
- **Red Flag:** If every performance issue triggers urgency instead of diagnosis, leadership is reacting instead of leading.
- **Key Question:** "Do we have a shared financial model that explains performance, and does everyone trust it?"

OPERATOR DIAGNOSTIC

Answer **Yes** or **No** to each question.

1. Is there one source of truth for eCommerce performance?
2. Do all teams agree on which metrics matter?
3. Is "great performance" clearly defined for this business?
4. Are activities consistently tied to financial outcomes?
5. Is the eCommerce strategy documented and understood?
6. Do teams present diagnoses and plans, not excuses?
7. Does leadership respond to volatility with clarity, not panic?
8. Is eCommerce's role in enterprise value clearly understood?

9. Are acquisition, conversion, and retention managed as one system?
10. Does leadership feel confident steering the digital business?

Scoring and Interpretation

Yes to 8–10 questions: The system is functioning as a unified engine.

Yes to 5–7 questions: The system is partially aligned but requires strengthening.

Yes to 0–4 questions: The system is fragmented and limiting growth.

Summary

The Growth Gap persists because leadership teams treat eCommerce as a project or initiative instead of a business unit. Without clear ownership, disciplined decision rights, and an operating cadence that links truth to action, teams default to committee-based strategy, activity-based KPIs, agency dependence, and reactive execution. The result is fatal: fragmented priorities, politicized metrics, and a system that cannot compound progress.

Closing the Growth Gap requires leadership to shift from managing outcomes to governing the system that produces outcomes.

Next, we move from symptoms to a deep dive into root causes by breaking down the Five Forces that keep brands stuck even when teams are working hard.

Part 1 Summary: From Symptoms to Root Causes

At this point, you should have some insight about one thing: In most cases, eCommerce companies are not struggling to succeed due to a lack of effort, talent, tools, or intent. Rather, eCommerce companies often struggle to achieve repeatable, profitable growth because the systems in place to govern eCommerce were never designed to support it.

The distinction between these two scenarios is imperative.

When a team sees results below expectations, the first response is typically to find a solution that fits within a tactical mindset. These solutions may seem productive. Unfortunately, they treat symptoms rather than addressing the root causes.

Additionally, when a team finds itself in this situation, it tends to assume the "engine" is fine and that the only way to achieve the desired results is to optimize the current systems rather than redesign them.

There is rarely an occasion when this assumption holds.

When an eCommerce company struggles to scale, the failure is systemic. There is no direction. The economics are misunderstood. There is no defined ownership of the process. The infrastructure cannot handle the workload. The demand being created is manufactured, not earned. These types of failures are not isolated to specific brands, categories, or business models. On the contrary, these failures occur in the same places, in the same order, across the board.

At this point, responsibility for resolving the issues needs to shift. No longer is the responsibility to correct the issues placed on the teams, nor is it placed on the agency, but instead it is placed squarely on the systems that support those teams and agencies.

Because if the system is misaligned, even great people will produce mediocre results. If the system is coherent, ordinary execution can outperform extraordinary effort trapped in chaos.

eCommerce outcomes are fragile due to the system's cross-functional nature, its sensitivity to economic conditions, and its dependence on speed. The system amplifies whatever organizational design and inputs it is given.

Part 2 is a diagnostic guide to identify the Five Forces of the eCommerce Growth Gap. It provides a framework for assessment rather than checklists or a menu of tactical recommendations.

Analyzing each of the Five Forces will help you determine whether your business has issues in any of these five fundamental components of success. If eCommerce isn't accomplishing its intended goals, you likely have a Strategy Gap (Force 1). If growth in eCommerce isn't creating corresponding growth in enterprise value, you likely have a Financial Linkages Gap (Force 2). If sound decisions aren't being converted into action, you likely have a Capability Gap (Force 3). If your operations can't scale to meet your goals, you likely have an Infrastructure Gap (Force 4). And if the market isn't recognizing and rewarding your eCommerce efforts at a sustainable cost, you likely have a Demand Gap (Force 5).

If part 1 provided evidence that your eCommerce organization has structural issues, part 2 will provide the identification of where the cracks in the foundation occur. Not to assign blame but to enable the resolution of the problems for good.

This is where our real work begins.

PART 2

WHY BRANDS GET STUCK

The Root Causes Behind Underperformance

THE FIVE FORCES THAT CREATE A GROWTH GAP

In every underperforming eCommerce business, the Growth Gap is created by a breakdown across five interdependent forces. These forces work together to determine whether digital activity translates into durable enterprise value or slowly erodes it.

The Five Forces are:

- The Strategy Gap: eCommerce lacks a clearly defined role, financial guardrails, or a plan that leadership has committed to.
- The Financial Linkages Gap: The economics of eCommerce are misunderstood, ignored, or disconnected from execution.

- The Capability & Organizational Gap: The organization lacks the ownership structures, decision rights, and expertise required to execute consistently.
- The Infrastructure & Process Gap: Technology, fulfillment, data, and operating processes cannot support the speed and quality the business requires.
- The Demand Generation Gap: Demand is manufactured rather than earned through a compounding engine.

Brands are generally not ignoring these forces completely. Instead, they typically invest too much time and resources in one or two of the Five Forces at the expense of the others.

The Growth Gap arises from incomplete development across all Five Forces rather than from a failure within a single force. Each force contributes to the organization's ability to deliver scalable, profitable eCommerce growth. It is crucial to understand each force individually and in relation to the others to build a complete, healthy system.

The primary purpose of the next several chapters will be to use the Five Forces to help define where your brand's leaders should direct their efforts to fix where the system is failing. The Five Forces will also illustrate why directing efforts and investments to only a portion of the system will yield fragile and unsustainable results.

COMMON eCOMMERCE FAILURE MODES

Failure Mode	Forces Invested	Forces Neglected	What It Looks Like
Red-Hot Money Loser	Demand Generation + Infrastructure & Operations	Strategy, Financial Linkages, Capabilities	Revenue is growing and the website looks great. Underneath, contribution margins are deteriorating, CAC is rising, and retention is weak. The business is manufacturing growth at a loss.
Big Hat, No Cattle	Strategy + Financial Linkages	Demand Generation, Capabilities, Infra-structure	The plan is sound and the economics are understood. But the organization cannot execute it. Decisions lack ownership, the team lacks bandwidth, and the road map stalls on contact with reality.
All Gas, No Map	Capabilities + Demand Generation	Strategy, Financial Linkages, Infrastruc-ture	The team is talented and marketing is active. But without strategic direction or financial guardrails, effort disperses across too many priorities. Growth is inconsistent and hard to explain.
Optimized for Irrelevance	Capabilities + Infra-structure & Operations	Strategy, Financial Linkages, Demand Generation	Operations run smoothly and the team executes well. But there is no demand engine and no clear strategic role for eCommerce. The business is opera-tionally excellent and commercially adrift.

Caption: Most brands recognize themselves in one of these patterns. The Growth Gap rarely comes from neglecting all five forces, but rather from overinvestment in one or two while ignoring the rest.

CHAPTER 6

Force 1: The Strategy Gap

Why Effort Without Direction Creates Drift

eCommerce does not fail all at once. It drifts.

Strategic drift occurs when a brand asks an eCommerce business to perform multiple functions simultaneously without establishing priorities or determining how it will weigh trade-offs. Many brands do this unknowingly.

They demand that eCommerce drives growth while also producing higher margins. They require that eCommerce maintain alignment with wholesale while also supporting inventory clearance. They believe that eCommerce can build the brand while also acting as the only fully controlled channel. They expect eCommerce to do all of this with greater speed and agility than any other channel.

None of these is incorrect or impossible on its own.

What needs to change is the belief that these objectives can be met simultaneously without an eCommerce strategy that defines how the organization will prioritize and fund them and how it will maintain alignment during times of stress.

For many brands, eCommerce has ambition but lacks definition. The distance between those two is our first of the Five Forces—the Strategy Gap, which is a root cause of the Growth Gap.

There are three consistent ways that the Strategy Gap appears.

1. The Wholesale DNA Trap

Most companies enter owned eCommerce with wholesale instincts developed long before embarking on the direct-to-consumer journey.

Wholesale trains leaders to achieve success through distribution and velocity. You develop products. You sell products in. You then rely on your retail partners to manage the customer experience, discounts, merchandising, and most of the operational complexity.

Once you move into owned eCommerce, the model gets flipped.

You now own the customer. You own the experience. You own the economics of discounting. You own the delivery, returns, service costs, fraud, payment fees, and the entire customer acquisition and retention process. You also own the immediate consequences of every decision.

However, most organizations continue to operate as if they do not.

They use the website as a catalog. They delay launches until the wholesale side is ready. They are hesitant to offer exclusive products, fearing they will betray their wholesale partners. They remain "diplomatic" with pricing and search to avoid upsetting their wholesale partners. They handcuff the distribution channel that could potentially provide them the most control, the most potential for profit margin upside, and the quickest feedback loop.

In this case, underperformance stems from misaligned identity, not channel limitations.

Said another way, a retail business cannot be adequately managed using a wholesale operating worldview.

2. eCommerce Role Confusion and the Refusal to Choose

Strategy failure in eCommerce often shows up as busy teams, expanding road maps, and goals that never quite align with financial reality because no one has defined what eCommerce is supposed to do for the business.

Not a revenue target. Not a "digital penetration" goal. Not a slide in a planning deck. A real strategy.

A real eCommerce strategy defines three things:

1. eCommerce's role in the overall enterprise
2. The value eCommerce is expected to create
3. The operating model required to deliver the desired outcomes

Without this definition, the organization will fill the gap with assumptions. Marketing views eCommerce as a growth engine, Finance wants eCommerce to be a margin engine, Merchandising expects eCommerce to be another sell-through lever, and Operations treats eCommerce like wholesale. Leadership wants all of these to be true at the same time. Every person is working hard, but no one is working toward the same goal.

The Growth Gap starts widening because the business is not aligned at the core.

Leaders say, "Grow eCommerce 30 percent," or "Become more digital," but those goals frequently have no relationship to unit economics, contribution margin, assortment strategy, operational realities, necessary capabilities, or the organization's actual capability to execute. As a result, targets become simply wishful thinking because they are not tied to any constraints.

A brand cannot expect full-price eCommerce discipline, wholesale parity, aggressive acquisition, and rapid inventory liquidation simultaneously without determining which objective must take a back seat when necessary.

Without a shared definition of eCommerce's role, every decision will be a negotiation. The work will expand. The priorities will change. The politics will overtake the collaboration.

What Misalignment Looks Like

When eCommerce lacks a meaningful definition, the signs within the business are consistent:

- **Decisions become reactionary.** The planning process devolves into a continuous cycle of weekly adjustments. Urgent issues take precedence over important issues. Leadership requests jump ahead in line. The backlog grows at a rate greater than the team can work through it.
- **Everything is a priority.** New initiatives are continually being added, and few are being removed. Sequencing is disappearing because there is no financial or strategic reasoning to guide the work.
- **Budgets start fighting rather than working together.** Finance is pulling back to protect margin. Marketing is pushing spend to

meet revenue requirements. Merchandising is pushing promotions to clear inventory. Operations is pushing the limits of constraints to protect fulfillment performance. Each function makes rational decisions based on its own objectives, but these decisions are irrational for the system.

- **Metrics are fragmenting the organization.** Each function is optimizing for its own metric. There is no single person accountable for the enterprise value.

These often appear to be execution problems, but they are upstream strategy problems.

A Clear Strategy Defines the Role of eCommerce

Until the role of eCommerce is defined, every discussion is going to be noise. High-performing brands define eCommerce across four roles. The roles are connected, and they need to be explicit:

- **Product:** eCommerce is the brand's most comprehensive and controlled representation of the assortment and communicates the product message as the brand fully intends it.
- **Content:** eCommerce engages, educates, and inspires. It shapes demand long before the customer reaches the cart.
- **Commerce:** eCommerce influences commercial outcomes across the ecosystem, online and offline. Even when the purchase happens elsewhere, the site often drives the decision.
- **Insights:** eCommerce generates first-party and behavioral data that enhance product development, marketing effectiveness, merchandising, and demand planning.

If a brand cannot articulate these roles, it does not have an eCommerce strategy. It has a website.

When eCommerce has been clearly defined and is being actively used to drive the business, the business achieves outcomes that matter beyond the eCommerce channel. They are as follows:

1. A premium, coherent brand experience
2. Incremental revenue with stronger margin and better mix

3. Better distribution, consumer connection, and resilience
4. Higher lifetime value and more efficient acquisition

These are enterprise value outcomes. If the organization is only optimizing for one outcome, generally revenue, then the strategy is incomplete by design.

3. The "Just Spend More" Delusion

When a strategy is absent, ad spending becomes the primary driver of results.

Ad spending is seen as a form of action. It produces activity that can be reported upward. It buys time, and at least for a while, it can even create a revenue bump.

After that, the math kicks in.

If the business has narrow contribution margins, paid acquisition cannot scale. If retention is weak, CAC inflation becomes fatal. If channel conflict leads to inconsistent pricing and promotions, conversion and LTV decline. If the organization lacks clear ownership and accountability, execution quality oscillates.

Spending more money exacerbates these problems rather than solving them.

That is why "spend more money" is such a dependable diagnostic. The organization is attempting to purchase growth without first developing the conditions under which growth is sustainable and repeatable.

The spend-more reflex exposes the absence of strategy.

The Real Source of Drift: Competing Versions of the Truth

Inside many brands, there exist simultaneous contradictory beliefs about eCommerce:

- "eCommerce should maximize margin" versus "eCommerce should increase brand awareness."
- "eCommerce should be sold at full price" versus "We must match the wholesale partner's promotional pricing so that we do not appear to be more expensive."

- "eCommerce should have the greatest selection available" versus "We should allocate the best inventory to our wholesale partners first."
- "We must invest aggressively in eCommerce growth" versus "We must improve eCommerce profitability immediately."
- "eCommerce is a supporting function" versus "eCommerce is a business unit with a P&L."

These may start as philosophical disagreements but quickly escalate to operational failure points. Ultimately, a business cannot be aligned behind target outcomes it does not agree upon.

What a Real Strategy Looks Like

Brands that run eCommerce well share three strategic characteristics:

1. **A documented, aligned definition of eCommerce's role.** Leadership has agreed on the role of eCommerce within the enterprise, the expected outcomes, and the constraints. The ambiguity is eliminated, and the trade-offs are intentional.
2. **Contribution-margin-based financial constraints.** The organization understands the profitability thresholds. The team knows the investment boundaries, and targets are based on unit economics, not wishes.
3. **A prioritized, sequenced road map that is aligned with outcomes.** The work is finite, and the sequencing is reasonable. The initiatives are linked to value creation, not noise or internal politics.

This represents the distinction between a strategy and a list of activities.

When an eCommerce strategy is not defined, teams work independently. The KPIs compete, the budgets conflict, and the execution slows. The system loses cohesion, and the Growth Gap accelerates.

When an eCommerce strategy is defined, the momentum returns. The speed of decision-making increases, road maps become actionable, and budgets work together. Teams stop negotiating and start building.

Closing the Strategy Gap is a performance accelerator.

CEO BRIEFING

Force 1: The Strategy Gap

- **Truth:** eCommerce underperforms when leadership refuses to choose. Asking the channel to maximize growth, margin, brand, wholesale harmony, and inventory clearance at the same time is not ambitious. It is strategic avoidance.
- **Red Flag:** If every major eCommerce decision requires negotiation across functions and no one can explain the primary objective of the channel in one sentence, the business does not have a strategy. It has competing agendas.
- **Key Question:** "What is eCommerce's primary role in our enterprise today, and what trade-offs have we explicitly agreed to make in order to support it?"

OPERATOR DIAGNOSTIC

Force 1: Do You Have a Real eCommerce Strategy?

Answer **Yes** or **No** to each question.

1. Can leadership articulate the primary role of eCommerce in one clear sentence?
2. Are the roles of eCommerce across product, content, commerce, and insights explicitly defined with agreed KPIs to measure progress?
3. Have growth, margin, and brand priorities been sequenced rather than pursued simultaneously?
4. Do marketing, merchandising, finance, and operations operate from the same definition of success?
5. Are financial targets grounded in contribution margin, not just revenue or ROAS?
6. Does eCommerce have the authority to make pricing, promotional, and assortment decisions aligned to its role?
7. Is the road map finite, sequenced, and tied directly to strategic outcomes rather than "requests"?
8. Do budgets follow strategy rather than react to short-term performance noise?
9. Can the team explain why spending should increase or decrease without referencing platforms or dashboards?

10. Are wholesale and eCommerce roles defined in a way that maximizes total enterprise value?

Scoring and Interpretation

Yes to 8–10 questions: Strategy is clear. Trade-offs are intentional. Execution has direction.

Yes to 5–7 questions: Strategy exists but is unstable. Competing priorities are still creating drag.

Yes to 0–4 questions: The Strategy Gap is a primary driver of underperformance. Effort will continue to produce drift.

Summary

The Strategy Gap is the absence of direction. Brands experiencing the Growth Gap rarely lack effort, tools, or ambition, but they often lack a coherent strategy that defines what the business is trying to become and how it will win. Without strategic clarity, teams chase disconnected initiatives, debate tactics, and optimize local performance while the system remains misaligned.

When strategy is vague, every idea feels valid, priorities clash, and eCommerce becomes reactive instead of intentional.

Next, we move from direction to truth by addressing the Financial Linkages Gap, the failure to understand and govern the economics that determine whether growth is truly profitable.

Case Study: The Strategy Gap

When eCommerce Is Asked to Be Everything at Once

The brand was a midsize footwear manufacturer with strong wholesale distribution and a growing direct-to-consumer channel. eCommerce represented roughly 12 percent of total revenue, but leadership believed it should be closer to 30 percent within three years. The category was competitive, but demand was healthy. The team was well funded, and the website was modern and functional.

From leadership's perspective, the problem seemed straightforward: eCommerce was "underperforming to its potential." The CEO wanted faster top-line growth, but finance wanted an improved contribution margin. The brand team wanted tighter storytelling and less discounting, and the sales team wanted eCommerce to support wholesale sell-through. The board wanted all of it, quickly. No one explicitly defined which objective mattered most.

Because the role of eCommerce was never clarified, execution became conflicted. The team was asked to scale acquisition aggressively while simultaneously reducing CAC. Promotions were launched to hit revenue targets, then pulled back to protect brand perception. Paid media was expected to drive growth but was constrained by ROAS targets. Inventory was bought to support growth scenarios that eCommerce had not committed to operationally. Each function was optimized for its own version of success.

Over time, the system destabilized. Road maps changed quarterly. Forecasts lost credibility. Teams spent more time defending priorities than executing them. When results missed expectations, leadership concluded the strategy needed to be "refreshed," which resulted in new goals layered on top of unresolved trade-offs.

The issue was that eCommerce had no defined mandate. It was simultaneously treated as a growth engine, a profit center, and a brand vehicle. Without a clear strategic role, every downstream decision became a negotiation, and every KPI became debatable.

This was the Strategy Gap at work.

CHAPTER 7

Force 2: The Financial Linkages Gap

When Dashboards Replace Economics

If the Strategy Gap is the absence of direction, the Financial Linkages Gap is the absence of shared truth. Brands experiencing an eCommerce Growth Gap rarely lack data. However, if they do not properly understand their economics, the outcomes are predictable. They arbitrarily set ROAS targets, artificially keep CAC expectations constant, suppress spending, and experience a chronic inability to scale profitably.

The business is flying without instruments. Decision-making that appears logical on a marketing dashboard becomes much less logical when viewed through the bank account. To close the Growth Gap, the organization needs to begin viewing eCommerce as a financial system and stop treating eCommerce as a marketing project.

This force manifests in three structural failures: financial blind spots, the missing eCommerce P&L, and improper pricing and promotion mechanics. Each failure and strategies for avoiding them are discussed next.

1. Financial Blind Spots

Most brands have dashboards full of KPIs, but they lack a model that translates those KPIs into economic truth and, ultimately, the P&L. The organization cannot clearly explain where profit is created, where it leaks, and what it costs to scale.

Contribution Margin, Variable Costs, and Bad Metrics

Every leadership team can tell you its gross revenue. Most teams can describe gross-to-net. Some can even recite their return rates from memory. However, ask most teams about the eCommerce contribution margin, and the room goes silent.

The contribution margin is the profit after the deduction of cost of goods sold (COGS) and all variable costs that affect the sale of a product. The contribution margin is the fundamental economic engine of a brand's ability to scale online. It establishes the relationship between CAC; payback windows; LTV; marketing investments; and ultimately, earnings before interest, taxes, depreciation, and amortization (EBITDA). The contribution margin is arguably the most critical metric in the eCommerce financials.

Unfortunately, most brands do not accurately measure their contribution margin because they do not model variable costs correctly (or at all).

Examples of variable costs include outbound shipping, pick and pack, credit card processing, platform fees, and transaction-based tools. These costs are frequently classified and obscured as overhead expenses versus variable expenses. Paid media is also typically treated as a fixed line item versus a variable lever.

Without accurate variable cost modeling, the contribution margin cannot be utilized to its fullest extent. Without consideration of the contribution margin, a break-even analysis cannot be completed. Without a break-even analysis, every ROAS target is nothing more than a guess or preference.

It then becomes clear why so many budget discussions seem arbitrary. The system lacks a governing truth.

There are predictable patterns when a brand fails to accurately track and report the contribution margin:

1. **Leaders reduce marketing spend too aggressively.** They suppress acquisition, at the exact moment it should expand, to chase "efficiency" without understanding how much variable profit is

being generated. They protect short-term ROAS at the expense of long-term scale.

2. **Brands scale channels that look efficient on paper.** Attribution exaggerates performance, spending increases, revenue grows, and eventually, finance recognizes that the scaled channels did not add any dollars to the bottom line.
3. **Growth problems get misdiagnosed**. Leaders isolate symptoms, such as "CAC is rising," but they cannot interpret the root cause ("Our variable costs compress margins; therefore, acquisition efficiency will always look worse than reality").
4. **Retention stays underfunded**. Teams overvalue last-click ROAS and undervalue lifecycle marketing. As such, email, short messaging service (SMS), and loyalty remain secondary programs, forcing the brand to repeatedly reacquire the same customers.
5. **Marketing budgets become constraints instead of levers**. Spending gets treated as fixed. The organization stops thinking about scale and starts thinking about containment. Teams optimize metrics instead of economics.

The brand shifts from "How big can this get?" to "What's the minimum we can spend without scaring anyone?"

That mindset is the Financial Linkages Gap in action.

The Linkage Chain Leaders Need to See

High-performing teams manage eCommerce through a simple linkage chain:

- Unit economics define contribution margin.
- Contribution margin defines break-even.
- Break-even and customer LTV define allowable CAC.
- Allowable CAC defines ROAS floors and spending range.
- Spending range defines growth capacity and EBITDA outcomes.

If the organization cannot connect those dots, the team will continue to debate tactics rather than truth.

Brands that fix these blind spots change fast. Leaders stop debating channels, creative assets, and attribution as if they are primary drivers of success. They begin making decisions based on economics. Spending becomes strategic instead of emotional, and KPIs become interpretable rather than political.

The shift looks like this:

- **From "ROAS targets" to "contribution margin guardrails":** ROAS becomes a tactical signal. The contribution margin becomes the strategic truth.
- **From "fixed CAC expectations" to "dynamic acquisition strategy tied to contribution margin and LTV":** CAC becomes elastic, expanding when the contribution margin is healthy and contracting when it's not.
- **From "budget as constraint" to "budget as a lever":** Spending is no longer something to protect. The budget becomes something to deploy with precision to drive variable profit.

Financial blind spots are rarely due to incompetence. They are due to organizational inheritance. eCommerce introduces a new economic language, whereas most midmarket brands are still speaking in wholesale terms.

Which leads to the second failure.

2. The Missing eCommerce P&L

Nearly every brand that struggles with eCommerce is operating using a partial or distorted P&L. Variable costs are either missing or incorrectly reported. Paid media is treated as fixed overhead. Fulfillment costs live in warehouse budgets. Customer service is buried under corporate expenses. Leaders present expense budgets and call them P&Ls.

A proper eCommerce P&L does not simply report performance. It should change how leaders think. The P&L turns noise into signal, activity into economics, ambition into a plan, and debate into decisions.

Absent a true eCommerce P&L, the business lives in two worlds—the world of KPIs and the world of financial outcomes—and they rarely intersect.

Far too many organizations treat the eCommerce P&L as an afterthought. Finance builds the company's main P&L, which is typically designed for wholesale economics, and eCommerce is squeezed into it. The eCommerce team treats annual expense budgets as profit statements. Leadership eventually settles for confusion and frustration.

Leaders often assume the numbers are trustworthy because they come from "the system." But the system wasn't built for eCommerce and cannot guide a retail business.

When a P&L is incomplete or inaccurate, the business consistently makes four damaging mistakes:

1. **The organization over- or underinvests in paid media because ROAS targets are arbitrary**. Either way, the business grows inefficiently.
2. **Leaders debate KPIs instead of contribution margin and unit economics.** Traffic, CVR, AOV, and ROAS become the center of every meeting. Each team fights for its metrics, but no one is fighting for the P&L.
3. **Leaders misdiagnose what drives EBITDA.** Leaders cannot answer basic questions like what break-even ROAS is, what the contribution margin is by category, or what the cost-to-serve constraints are. As a result, decisions drift away from financial reality.
4. **The organization runs the business top-down or bottom-up, but not both.** Either the leadership team sets financial expectations with no operational path to achieve them, or the team builds KPI forecasts with no connection to achievable margin. Both models break.

When leaders see a true eCommerce P&L for the first time, key realizations are unlocked and hit fast:

- "We aren't being aggressive enough, and therefore we're leaving growth on the table."
- "Our economics, not our tactics, are the constraint."
- "Our KPI planning and financial outcomes are two different worlds."

This is the moment the room gets quiet—because everyone realizes the barrier to scale was never the algorithm or the agency (or other misidentified factor). It was the P&L.

Once a proper P&L exists, the organization operates in a completely different manner.

Team members move from reactive scramble to proactive planning. Fire drills disappear. Leaders stop chasing weekly ROAS fluctuations and start planning the model three, six, and twelve months out.

Team members stop debating ROAS and start discussing contribution margin. Marketing loses the burden of "fixing growth" alone. Finance gains visibility., the operations team understands how cost-to-serve affects scale, and conversations become aligned.

Budget discussions become calmer, more rational, and more strategic. When the economics are clear, the budget is no longer a battleground and instead becomes a powerful lever.

Teams plan the business top-down and bottom-up. Top-down: "Here is the EBITDA, contribution margin, and revenue we will achieve." Bottom-up: "Here are the weekly KPIs required to achieve that, and here is what must be true operationally to support them." The two finally connect.

A clean P&L does not create discipline. It *enables* discipline. A clean P&L gives the business a reliable source of truth. It replaces assumptions with structure, noise with clarity, and opinion with economics.

Then one more truth becomes unavoidable.

3. Improper Pricing and Promotion Mechanics

Pricing decisions determine the contribution margin, the contribution margin determines allowable CAC, and allowable CAC determines whether paid acquisition can scale. When pricing is undisciplined, the system breaks even if everything else looks healthy. This is one of the fastest ways the Growth Gap widens without leadership realizing why.

Where Wholesale Instincts Destroy Retail Math

If there is one area where wholesale-heritage brands routinely underestimate eCommerce complexity, it is pricing.

Most leadership teams fully understand wholesale pricing. They live in a world of margin dollars, trade discounts, volume commitments, and negotiated programs. However, when they transition to eCommerce, they subconsciously apply the same wholesale logic.

In wholesale, discounts live upstream in negotiated trade terms. In eCommerce, discounts are taken directly off the manufacturer's suggested retail price (MSRP). Every percentage point compresses the contribution margin immediately—and often invisibly if the P&L is incomplete.

Yet many organizations treat promotions like marketing tactics instead of economic events that affect the P&L.

Average unit retail (AUR) deteriorates. Margin collapses. Consumers learn bad habits. Wholesale partners get irritated. Leadership misreads the signals.

Product cost remains the same in wholesale and eCommerce, but the math stops there. Understanding product economics and the price architecture that supports them is one of the most important capabilities missing in brands experiencing a Growth Gap.

The Three Ways Brands Break Their Own Margins

Three common pitfalls contribute to pricing errors:

1. **Discounting addiction:** Promotions become the go-to tactic to deliver short-term revenue. The intention is good. "Move inventory," "make our plan," and "capitalize on demand." The long-term impact is detrimental. Consumers learn to wait. Perception of brand value declines. CAC rises as conversion quality falls. Margin structure deteriorates. Once you teach the consumer to wait for a discount, you cannot easily unteach it.
2. **Avoiding consumer-centric levers because the team is stuck in wholesale mode:** Brands refuse to use levers that reduce friction and improve conversion because they feel like "costs." The clearest example is shipping. Consumers hate paying for shipping. It's one of the strongest conversion levers in eCommerce. But brands often resist offering free shipping because they perceive outbound freight as an unacceptable cost rather than a strategic investment that increases CVR, AOV, and LTV.

3. **Allowing wholesale partners to dictate promotion cadence and minimum advertised price (MAP):** Retail pressure drives discount windows and pricing precedent. This creates channel conflict, consumer confusion, and internal politics. When owned eCommerce is the only full-price option online, it becomes a consumer IQ test. And consumers pass every time by finding the lowest price somewhere else.

The Organizational Consequences of Failure to Properly Manage Pricing

Pricing failures don't just affect the margin line. They reshape behavior across the business.

1. **Leadership misinterprets the signals.** The teams see revenue spikes and assume promotions "worked." They see margin declines and misdiagnose marketing efficiency issues. Teams question paid media instead of the pricing structure. They conflate discount-driven revenue with healthy demand.
2. **Wholesale and sales teams complain.** Every wholesale team has said some version of "eCommerce isn't as profitable as wholesale." The statement is almost always wrong, but the frustration is legitimate. When eCommerce pricing is inconsistent, ad hoc, or poorly communicated, every retail partner feels the ripple effects.
3. **Consumers become confused or discouraged.** Pricing inconsistency creates hesitation. Promotional overuse trains customers to wait to purchase, and underuse frustrates them. Incoherent MAP signals instability. Confusion is one of the fastest ways to kill conversion and LTV.

When a brand properly and deliberately manages pricing strategy, AUR stabilizes, promotions become intentional, contribution margin strengthens, wholesale tension decreases, and marketing and finance operate from the same model. The growth engine becomes more predictable. Pricing discipline is not just a merchandising task. It is a Growth Gap prevention system.

CEO BRIEFING

Force 2: The Financial Linkages Gap

- **Truth:** eCommerce does not underperform because ROAS is wrong. It underperforms because KPIs are being used as a substitute for understanding the contribution margin and the real P&L. When leaders manage dashboards instead of economics, the business optimizes activity instead of profit.
- **Red Flag:** If leadership debates whether CAC is "too high" without being able to explain the break-even contribution margin, allowable CAC, and payback logic, the organization is operating without a financial model. Decisions may feel disciplined, but they are structurally blind.
- **Key Question:** "Do we have a single, trusted financial model in the form of a P&L that clearly links unit economics, contribution margin, CAC, spend range, and EBITDA, and do we actively use it to make investment decisions?"

OPERATOR DIAGNOSTIC

Force 2: Are Financial Blind Spots Driving the Growth Gap?

Answer **Yes** or **No** to each question.

1. Do we know our true contribution margin after all variable cost-to-serve expenses?
2. Are outbound shipping, fulfillment, payment fees, platform fees, and transaction costs modeled as variable, not overhead, costs?
3. Is paid media treated as a variable investment tied to the contribution margin and LTV rather than a fixed budget?
4. Can leadership clearly explain our break-even contribution margin and break-even ROAS?
5. Do CAC targets flex based on margin health and customer value?
6. Do we plan the business both top-down from financial outcomes and bottom-up from operational KPIs?
7. Do budget discussions start with economics rather than ROAS or channel performance?
8. Are pricing and promotional decisions evaluated based on their impact on the contribution margin?

9. Can we explain why spending should increase or decrease without referencing attribution models?
10. Do marketing, finance, merchandising, and operations trust the same financial model?

Scoring and Interpretation

Yes to 8–10 questions: Financial clarity is strong. Spending is a lever, not a constraint. Scale is intentional.

Yes to 5–7 questions: Partial visibility exists, but blind spots are still limiting confidence and growth.

Yes to 0–4 questions: The Financial Linkages Gap is a primary constraint. Performance will remain unstable regardless of tactical execution.

Summary

The Financial Linkages Gap is the absence of shared truth. Brands rarely lack data, but many lack a trusted financial model that connects KPIs, unit economics, contribution margin, break-even logic, CAC, spending range, and EBITDA. When dashboards replace economics, ROAS becomes a proxy for profitability, budgets become political, and growth becomes constrained by fear rather than governed by math.

Once the economics are visible and shared, decisions become calmer, spending becomes strategic, and teams stop debating tactics and start managing the business.

Next, we address the execution layer by examining the Capability and Organizational Gap, the structural failures that prevent good decisions from turning into consistent action.

Case Study: The Financial Linkages Gap

When Revenue Grows but Profit Doesn't Follow

The sporting goods brand had what most executives would call a "successful" eCommerce business. Revenue was growing year over year, traffic was up, and ROAS targets were being met. The marketing dashboards appeared healthy, and the channel regularly met its top-line target.

And yet, the P&L told a different story.

Despite revenue growth, the contribution margin and EBITDA were shrinking. Cash flow was tightening. Promotions were becoming more frequent, shipping costs were rising, and returns were creeping upward. Finance flagged the issue repeatedly, but the warnings were vague: "Margins are under pressure," or "eCommerce profitability is soft." No one could explain precisely why.

Marketing pointed to strong ROAS and a stable CAC. The eCommerce team cited revenue growth and improved conversion rates. Finance pointed to a declining contribution margin but lacked a model that the rest of the organization trusted. Each function was technically correct when viewing the P&L through its own lens, but the business lacked a shared economic truth.

ROAS became the proxy for financial health. As long as campaigns hit the target ROAS, spending was approved. However, those targets were set arbitrarily based on benchmarks without fully accounting for the business's COGS, discount depth, fulfillment costs, return rates, or customer LTV. Paid media appeared efficient while the system quietly leaked margin everywhere else.

When bottom-line results tightened, leadership reacted by policing spending more aggressively. Prospecting budgets were cut to improve the short-term margin. Retention investment was deferred. Promotions were used to backfill revenue gaps. Each move temporarily stabilized one metric while worsening another, and the bottom line of the P&L oscillated instead of compounding.

The core failure was not that teams ignored finance. It was that the business never agreed on a shared definition of the contribution margin or how eCommerce created value. Economics were reviewed after the fact, vaguely, and not used as a governing input for decisions.

This is the Financial Linkages Gap in action.

Anatomy of an eCommerce P&L

The eCommerce P&L is designed to provide a clear answer to two questions:

1. Does each incremental order create value or destroy it?
2. Do our actions and KPIs translate to financial outcomes?

Following is a best-practice eCommerce P&L you can use for a comparison with how your team currently measures and reviews the financial performance of your eCommerce business.

A downloadable version of this P&L template is available at toolkit.ecommercegrowthgap.com.

Line Item	$	% of Net	Notes
Gross Merchandise Sales	$11,500,000	112.7%	The "Top Line" vanity number
Returns & Discounts	($1,500,000)	14.7%	The "Leaky Bucket" most marketers ignore
Shipping Revenue	$200,000	2.0%	Money collected from the consumer for shipping
Net Revenue	**$10,200,000**	**100.0%**	**The true starting point**
COGS			
Product Cost	$3,500,000	34.3%	Landed product cost
Shipping Expense	$1,224,000	12.0%	Outbound freight to customer costs
Total COGS	$4,724,000	46.3%	Total Cost of Goods Sold
Product Margin	$6,700,000	65.7%	Margin on Product Only
Gross Profit	**$5,476,000**	**53.7%**	**Your "Fuel" for growth**
Variable Selling Costs			
Distribution & Fulfillment	$400,000	3.9%	Often a hidden growth killer
Merchant & Platform Fees	$250,000	2.5%	Non-negotiable tax or growth
Packaging & Consumables	$50,000	0.5%	Part of the customer experience
Total Variable Selling Costs	$700,000	6.9%	The "System" Costs
Variable Marketing Costs		0.0%	
Paid Media (FB/Google/TikTok)	$1,600,000	15.7%	Performance-based spend
Affiliate/Influencer Comm	$400,000	3.9%	Performance-based spend
Total Variable Marketing Costs	$2,000,000	19.6%	The "Gas" in the engine
Contribution Margin	**$2,776,000**	**27.2%**	**The "Truth" Line**
Fixed Operating Expenses			
eCommerce Staff (Payroll)	$600,000	5.9%	Capability costs
SaaS & Infrastructure	$200,000	2.0%	Technology and Mar tech costs
Agency Retainers	$250,000	2.5%	External capability
Fixed Marketing Fees	$100,000	1.0%	SEO, Brand, PR, Creative, etc.
Functional Allocations	$100,000	1.0%	HR, IT, Finance, etc.
Total Fixed Operating Expenses	$1,250,000	12.3%	
Operating Income (EBITDA)	**$1,526,000**	**15.0%**	**What goes to the bank**

CHAPTER 8

Force 3: The Capability and Organizational Gap

Why Great People Still Lose in Bad Systems

If the Strategy Gap is about direction and the Financial Linkages Gap is about truth, the Capability and Organizational Gap is about execution.

Behind the dashboards and debates, nearly every struggling brand shares the same underlying issue: The organization running eCommerce is not designed to win.

The eCommerce organization is usually understaffed, and there is a lack of clear ownership. The teams responsible for executing are overwhelmed with hands-on-keys work and starved of strategy. Decision-making moves from those closest to the work to those furthest from it. The organization is very busy, but it is not effective, and therefore, confidence is lost.

This is not a capability problem in the traditional sense. Rather, it is a design problem, a business unit problem, and a leadership and ownership problem.

eCommerce is a retail business unit with dozens of interconnected levers, yet most brands approach it as if it were simply a marketing function. That discrepancy is where the Growth Gap compounds.

This force manifests in four execution failures: ownership, governance, decision-making, and throughput. These failures are often mistaken for truth problems, but that is a misdiagnosis. The economics may be known, the data may be available, and the insights may be evident. What is lacking is the organization's machinery to turn decisions into action.

In the following sections, we will dismantle the misconception that "increasing head count" solves the Growth Gap and explore how to restructure the business unit for ownership, reclaim your strategy from external partners, and transform data into a tool for speed.

1. No True eCommerce Owner

The most consistent pattern across underperforming brands is simple: No one owns eCommerce, or the assigned "owner" lacks the authority, seniority, or experience to run a retail P&L. The channel is essentially ungoverned and turns into a committee-based effort.

There are numerous consequences:

1. No one is accountable for results. Everyone touches the channel, but no one owns the outcome. When performance softens, blame is dispersed. Marketing blames the budget. The product department blames the inventory department. The team blames the agency. Leadership blames the strategy. The organization becomes a circle of finger-pointing.
2. Strategy gets set by committee. Without a leader to define the strategic priorities, every function develops its own plan. Merchandising sets one direction. Marketing sets another. Finance imposes a third and Operations adds a fourth. The business plan becomes an accumulation of preferences rather than a coherent strategy.
3. Decision rights move upward and outward. Individuals closest to the work stop making decisions. All major decisions are escalated to higher levels of the organization. Speed becomes impossible, and the work is reduced to negotiation.
4. Confidence erodes at the top. Boards and executives lose faith in the eCommerce team's ability to execute. They stop trusting forecasts. They question the team's investment decisions. In some cases, they conclude that "eCommerce doesn't work for our brand" without ever acknowledging that leadership is the constraint, not the channel itself. This is the worst consequence of all because

without faith in the eCommerce team, the executive team reduces eCommerce investments, thereby accelerating the Growth Gap.

2. Agency Overdependence

Most brands don't realize they have an agency problem until the damage is already done. The challenge is not that the agencies are incompetent or malevolent. Simply put, when the internal team is unable to lead, the agency serves as the operating system.

Agencies are designed to optimize channels. Brands are designed to grow companies. Although these two goals intersect, they are not the same. When leaders lose sight of this fact, agencies quietly begin to take on the responsibilities of the internal team, and they sometimes even take on the responsibilities of the leadership team.

Every brand starts with good intentions. Agencies are hired to provide support for execution, increase bandwidth, and bring specialization. Agency overdependency, then, is not the result of the internal team being less capable than the agencies but of the organization's failure to establish who will govern priorities, sequencing, and trade-offs. When the organization fails to establish a single internal owner, agencies fill the void by default. This can manifest in a few ways:

1. **Ambassadors of prioritization.** Agencies begin to develop the organization's priorities. They will recommend budgets, define best practices, suggest road maps, and dictate the pace of progress. The agency's generic strategy becomes the organization's de facto strategy, regardless of whether it is based on contribution margin, inventory realities, or operational limitations.
2. **Optimizers of siloed KPIs.** ROAS, spending efficiency, platform performance, A/B tests, and channel benchmarks are not the same as profit. Even a high-performing agency can steer the business wrong if the governing metric is wrong. And agencies rarely see or understand the numbers that matter most on the P&L.
3. **Trust in dashboards over economics.** Agency reporting looks authoritative. Complex graphs and sophisticated attribution logic can create the impression that insightful decisions are being made.

However, if the reporting does not link to the P&L, the reporting is noise that appears intelligent.

Why Agencies Get Misaligned (Even When They're Good)

Most agency teams are not attempting to mislead anyone. Structural problems are the primary reason for the misalignment.

Agencies are paid to optimize channels, not the contribution margin. Their incentive is to drive activity: more campaigns, more creative work, more spending. Activity is easy to measure. Profit is not.

In short, agencies are incentivized by activity, not outcomes. More complexity creates more scope for the agency, and more scope means more revenue. Only a few agencies are compensated for increasing variable profit or decreasing cost-to-serve.

Agencies don't see, or don't understand, the full eCommerce P&L. They don't control inventory, promotions, customer service, or fulfillment. Agencies don't see variable costs or merchandising delays. Without this context, even the smartest agency recommendations can be structurally wrong.

Agencies are not the cause of the Growth Gap. But without alignment, they can accelerate it.

Put simply: A brand cannot outsource strategy in a business system as complex as eCommerce.

When agency alignment is fixed, value is quickly unlocked:

1. Reporting becomes crystal clear and focused on what matters. The noise disappears. Reports transition from platform metrics to actionable insights. Everyone starts talking about the contribution margin, the break-even ROAS, the CAC:LTV ratio, and financial outcomes, not meaningless dashboard fluctuations.
2. The internal team drives the agenda. Agencies revert to their proper place: supporting execution, not setting direction. The team stops reacting to agency suggestions and starts orchestrating the business.
3. Agencies finally add value. The best agencies thrive within structure. When the brand sets strategy and provides clarity, agencies can focus on what they do best: bringing capability, specialization,

efficiency, and bandwidth. They stop adding noise and start adding lift.

Agencies can be powerful accelerators, but only if the brand leads. When agencies define the road map, the business loses connection to the P&L. When the internal team takes ownership, the entire system becomes coherent.

eCommerce is far too complex, interdependent, and sensitive to financial factors to outsource strategy. Agencies should serve to turbocharge the operating model rather than define it.

3. Data Dysfunction

Counterintuitively, data dysfunction does not stem from a lack of information. Brands may track everything, but they often lack a governing system that connects metrics to the contribution margin and clear decision rights.

As a result, dashboards become debate tools rather than decision tools. Teams spend more time analyzing performance than improving it. The business appears analytical on the surface, but underneath, execution slows and is still largely based on opinions and instincts.

Why Dashboards Don't Create Insight

The quiet truth behind the Growth Gap is that many brands today are data rich and insight poor. They are drowning in dashboards that don't match, reports that lack context, and "analytics theater" where opinions are disguised as insights.

They have stacks of dashboards, reports, scorecards, channel metrics, platform metrics, and spreadsheet after spreadsheet, all telling different stories. The charts don't match. Definitions differ. Trends contradict. Meetings become debates about what is "true" instead of decisions about what actions to take.

Data dysfunction creates decision paralysis or chaos. When teams don't trust the system, they either freeze or spiral, and endless debates start replacing momentum. In essence, teams usually know what's happening, but they cannot act on it with confidence.

The Illusion of Being "Data-Driven"

Walk into any weekly eCommerce meeting, and you'll see the problem immediately. The team reviews platform dashboards. The agency shows performance graphs. Finance references yet another report. Merchandising brings last week's sell-through. Someone else presents Shopify numbers.

This is the defining pattern of a data-dysfunctional organization: It *feels* data-driven. It *looks* data-driven. But it's actually a carefully staged theater of analytics.

The real decisions are made by instinct, politics, or panic. Not insight. The symptoms are unmistakable:

1. **Endless debate, zero direction.** Teams argue about ROAS definitions, attribution windows, incrementality methods, email attribution, and discount impact. Everything except what matters. The debate becomes the work.
2. **Too many dashboards, no source of truth.** Agency metrics do not match platform data. Platform data do not match finance data. Each function uses the numbers that support its agenda.
3. **Metrics without meaning.** Teams review traffic, CVR, AOV, ROAS, click-through rate (CTR), cost per click (CPC), and open rates without connecting any of them to the contribution margin, break-even economics, customer value, or EBITDA.
4. **Forecasting becomes guesswork.** Budget planning becomes emotional. Resource allocations become reactionary. Forecasts swing wildly. No one can explain last month with confidence.

The issue is not data availability or access, but rather the absence of a disciplined Data → Insight → Action cycle rooted in financial reality.

Why These Problems Persist

You'd think with so much data, brands would be smarter. The opposite is often true.

Three root causes drive the dysfunction:

1. **Lack of true analytical capability and rigor:** Anyone can pull reports. Few can extract insight. Most eCommerce teams are staffed with smart, hardworking operators but lack analytical depth. Analysts understand how to ask questions of the data, identify trends and patterns, create models, and relate trends to economic conditions. Without an analyst, dashboards become decorative. However, hiring a data scientist alone won't solve this problem. The organization must also create conditions where data and analysts can inform the truth, even when that truth is difficult for marketing, merchandising, or C-suite teams to accept.
2. **No single source of truth:** Data live everywhere: Shopify, agencies, ad platforms, email service providers (ESPs), business intelligence (BI) tools, finance systems, attribution models, and more. When there is no single system that is considered authoritative, every team member uses the data that supports their position. If there is no agreed-upon truth, teams will create their own.
3. **The wrong metrics are emphasized:** Brands focus on the metrics that are easiest to measure rather than the metrics that are most important. ROAS instead of contribution margin. Open rate instead of LTV. Traffic instead of product economics. Sessions instead of merchandising impact. If the financial linkages are lacking, the metrics will always point the business in the wrong direction.

What Happens When the Data Dysfunction Is Fixed

When a brand establishes a disciplined Data → Insight → Action cycle, the transformation is both immediate and noticeable:

1. **Less debate, more alignment.** The team stops debating the numbers and begins asking more intelligent questions. Meetings

shorten, decisions occur rapidly, and debates improve. Alignment also improves because the truth is visible.

2. **Leaders see true performance.** Data no longer serve as a weapon but as a mirror. Suddenly, the organization can see which channels are driving the business. Which products create or erode margin? Where are the true conversion bottlenecks? What is causing CAC to rise or decline? How is retention performing? The organization transitions from guessing to knowing.
3. **Dashboards become a tool, not a burden.** Reports stop being overwhelming. Dashboards stop being performative. Data become clarity, not chaos.

When the Data → Insight → Action cycle exists, debate collapses into alignment. Leaders stop asking "Is this number right?" and start asking "What should we do next?"

4. The Velocity Trap (Busy Versus Fast)

Most eCommerce teams don't think they're slow. They believe they are overwhelmed. They believe they are under-resourced. They believe they are constantly fighting fires. However, "busy" is not the same as "fast."

Slowness in eCommerce rarely looks like people doing nothing. It usually looks like the following:

- Decision bottlenecks and consensus loops
- Weeks to launch obvious tests
- Extended waiting for approvals and inputs
- Agency dependence, slowing execution
- Road-map whiplash
- Creative cycles dragging because briefs are unclear
- Leaders escalating tactical requests, inserting themselves because they don't trust the system
- Far too many initiatives underway and none executed well

Slowness is systemic. It emerges when the organization lacks clarity about what matters, who decides, and why. Everything appears important, and nothing is constrained. The calendar is filled with activity but devoid of results. Real velocity in eCommerce is about finishing the right work sooner. Velocity is a throughput problem, not a hustle problem.

When the strategy is vague, every idea is valid. When roles are fuzzy, everyone weighs in. When priorities are unclear, everything feels urgent. When everything is urgent, everything slows.

This matters because eCommerce is speed-sensitive. Demand shifts quickly. Inventory risk is real. Competitors move fast. Customers expect immediacy. A slow team bleeds revenue, trades margin for the wrong kind of urgency, and becomes more promotional than necessary.

Healthy speed is not chaos. It is constrained, aligned throughput. The team becomes faster by thinking better: fewer priorities, clearer owners, trusted data, and decision rights close to the work.

What Happens When the Organization Is Designed Correctly

Even when brands have capable people, organizational design often sets them up to fail. Most eCommerce teams are overloaded with execution and under-resourced in strategy. They are excellent at getting things done but lack the time, space, or authority to decide what should be done.

When the right eCommerce leader, capabilities, and organizational design are in place, the business environment changes almost immediately:

- **Leadership becomes confident again.** Forecasts make sense. Plans feel credible. Discussions shift from panic to prioritization. Boards stop questioning the channel and start supporting it.
- **Priorities become clearer.** The noise quiets. The work aligns. The team knows what matters, why it matters, and how it connects to contribution margin.
- **KPIs start improving.** Not because the team suddenly became more talented but because it is finally working on the real constraints rather than reacting to the loudest problems.

When a true eCommerce owner is in place, the business becomes focused and confident. That emotional shift is not a side effect. It is the signal that the system is beginning to work.

Why Capability and Organizational Design Are a Force

eCommerce is a cross-functional sport. No single function can deliver it alone. Without a leader to orchestrate it, the system breaks.

The Growth Gap thrives in environments where ownership is unclear and teams are trapped in endless execution. It closes when someone is accountable for aligning the work, sequencing initiatives, connecting actions to KPIs, and connecting KPIs to financial outcomes.

When capability and organizational design are aligned, the business environment changes quickly:

- Leadership confidence returns because plans become credible.
- Road maps stabilize because priorities are governed, not negotiated.
- Agencies add lift instead of noise because the brand leads.
- Meetings produce decisions because truth is shared.
- Velocity increases because work in progress is constrained and owners are empowered.

This is the real revelation: Talent finally looks talented because the system no longer sabotages it.

CEO BRIEFING

Force 3: The Capability and Organizational Gap

- **Truth:** eCommerce underperforms not because teams lack talent, data, or effort but because the organization is not designed to convert decisions into execution. When ownership is unclear, agencies govern by default, data stall decisions, and velocity collapses.
- **Red Flag:** If eCommerce feels busy but slow, if agencies shape priorities, if meetings debate data instead of deciding action, and if confidence erodes upward to the board, this is not a performance issue. It is an operating system failure.
- **Key Question:** "Do we have clear ownership, decision rights, and execution constraints that allow good decisions to turn into action quickly and repeatedly?"

OPERATOR DIAGNOSTIC

Force 3: Is the Capability and Organizational Gap Preventing Execution?

Answer **Yes** or **No** to each question.

Ownership and Governance

1. Is there a single, clearly accountable eCommerce owner with authority to run the channel as a business unit? Is that leader senior enough to command cross-functional alignment?
2. Does that owner have decision rights over priorities, sequencing, and trade-offs, not just execution?
3. Are decision rights clearly documented so that teams know who decides and who contributes?
4. Do major eCommerce decisions get made by accountable owners rather than by committee?

Agency Role and Control

5. Do agencies operate inside a brand-defined strategy, road map, and economic guardrails?
6. Are agencies evaluated on their ability to support outcomes, not just channel metrics or activity?
7. Does the internal team set priorities and cadence rather than reacting to agency recommendations?
8. Can the internal team confidently challenge agency recommendations using business context and constraints?

Data and Decision Systems

9. Is there a single, trusted source of truth used to make decisions across functions?
10. Do meetings consistently convert data into decisions and actions rather than succumbing to debate and reanalysis?
11. Are the primary metrics reviewed directly connected to the contribution margin and business outcomes?
12. Can the team explain what changed, why it changed, and what action will follow without unnecessary escalation?

Velocity and Throughput

13. Are priorities stable enough that teams can finish work instead of constantly restarting?
14. Is work in progress intentionally constrained so that the team is not running too many initiatives at once?
15. Are owners empowered to move work forward without excessive approvals or consensus loops?
16. Do tests, campaigns, and website changes launch quickly once a decision is made?

Organizational Health

17. Do teams understand why they are doing each major initiative?
18. Does leadership trust forecasts, road maps, and delivery timelines?
19. Does eCommerce feel fast, focused, and deliberate rather than busy and reactive?
20. Does the organization feel confident in its ability to execute repeatedly, not just occasionally?

Scoring and Interpretation

Yes to 16–20 questions: Your organization is structurally capable. Execution converts clarity into results. Velocity compounds advantage.

Yes to 11–15 questions: Partial capability. Execution works, but friction, agency influence, or data noise is slowing throughput.

Yes to 6–10 questions: Systemic execution drag. Ownership, governance, and decision systems are misaligned.

Yes to 0–5 questions: The Capability and Organizational Gap is a primary driver of underperformance. Talent is being wasted by design.

Summary

The Capability and Organizational Gap is the execution breakdown that occurs when the eCommerce business unit is not designed to win. Without a true owner, decision rights collapse into committees, agencies govern by default, data stall decisions, and teams become busy but slow. Even with a clear strategy and economic truth, performance remains fragile if the organization lacks the machinery to convert decisions into action.

Regardless of how strong the team is, execution fails when ownership, governance, and throughput are unclear.

Next, we examine the scalability layer by addressing the Infrastructure and Process Gap, the hidden operational and technical constraints that quietly cap profitable growth.

Case Study: The Capability and Organizational Gap

When Everyone Is Busy and No One Owns the Outcome

On paper, the midmarket electronics brand was well resourced. The eCommerce team had grown steadily over several years as the company invested in the channel. Agencies were in place across media, creative, conversion rate optimization (CRO), and customer relationship management (CRM). Specialists owned individual functions, and weekly meetings were full.

Despite the investment, performance felt fragile. Decisions moved slowly, initiatives stalled, and priorities changed midcycle. When results missed expectations, leadership heard the same explanations repeatedly: Approvals took too long, dependencies weren't cleared, or another team owned the constraint. Work happened everywhere, but ownership lived nowhere.

The organization had talent, but it lacked capability.

Responsibility was distributed by function rather than by outcome. The marketing team owned acquisition. The brand team owned creative assets. The merchandising team owned assortment. The operations team owned fulfillment. The finance team owned margins. And eCommerce sat in the middle, accountable for the number but unable to govern the inputs that produced it.

As pressure increased, consensus and chaos culture took over. Decisions required alignment from too many stakeholders, so they were either delayed or escalated. Agencies filled the vacuum by driving road maps based on their own incentives. Internal teams reacted rather than executed. The loudest voice in the room often won, regardless of economic impact.

No one could clearly answer a simple question: "Who owns this decision?"

The absence of clear decision rights created predictable behavior. Teams protected their own KPIs. Cross-functional tension increased. Meetings multiplied. Execution slowed precisely when speed mattered most. When performance improved, it was due to heroics. When it declined, accountability blurred.

This brand had a glaring Capability and Organizational Gap.

CHAPTER 9

Force 4: The Infrastructure and Process Gap

Why Broken Plumbing Caps Profitable Growth

If the Strategy Gap is about direction, the Financial Linkages Gap is about truth, and the Capability and Organizational Gap is about execution, the Infrastructure and Process Gap is about whether the business can scale what it is trying to do.

Beneath the surface, almost every struggling brand is fighting its own internal machinery. The tech stack is a "spaghetti" of legacy code or an overbuilt maze of unused apps. The warehouse, built for wholesale pallets rather than parcel speed, is hemorrhaging margin through cost-to-serve inefficiencies. The operating rhythm is nonexistent, replaced by a "fire-drill" culture where teams react to noise rather than following a road map.

This is the part that leadership teams underestimate because it isn't glamorous. It doesn't show up in campaign recaps, creative reviews, or marketing debates. It shows up quietly, below the line, in cost-to-serve, in delivery promises, in returns processing, in site speed, in failed integrations, and in the weekly chaos that makes even competent teams feel like they're pushing a boulder uphill.

In other words, this force is the execution substrate. It is the gap between a brand's digital ambition and its physical and technical reality. Even the most talented team, armed with a perfect strategy, cannot scale a business that relies on manual heroics and broken plumbing.

eCommerce is a high-velocity business system that requires frictionless transmission to move. When the infrastructure is misaligned, the "engine" revs, but the wheels don't turn. Speed becomes a liability, complexity becomes a tax, and the Growth Gap widens because the business literally cannot move fast enough to keep up with the market.

In the following sections, we will dismantle the myth that "better marketing" can outrun "bad plumbing." Instead, we will look at how to audit your cost-to-serve, simplify your tech stack into a growth lever, and install the operating rhythm (the "heartbeat") required to turn chaotic activity into predictable momentum.

1. Operational Constraints

Operational constraints define the upper limit of your growth. You can generate demand, sharpen your positioning, and increase spending, but if the physical system behind the business cannot deliver efficiently, profitability will compress, and momentum will stall.

It is easy to miss how quickly cost-to-serve friction compounds. Small inefficiencies across shipping, fulfillment, returns, and customer service accumulate and, over time, become the hidden ceiling on scale.

Why Operational Reality Sets Your Ceiling

Most brands underestimate the amount of operational friction that is consuming their profit margins. They will spend hours debating whether ROAS should be 2.5 or 3.0, reforecast acquisition weekly, and obsess over creative fatigue. Then they will spend ten minutes examining the line items that are quietly eating away at the profit margin more than any marketing lever: Outbound shipping. Pick and pack. Packaging. Split shipments. Returns. Customer service workflows. Warehouse accuracy. Delivery times.

These components should not be written off as boring back-office details. They form the operating spine of the eCommerce model, and when they're weak, the entire engine slows down while the economics compress.

The irony is that for many eCommerce organizations, outbound freight becomes one of the highest costs in the eCommerce P&L after the product itself. Returns can easily consume 10 to 15 percent of gross revenue in some categories. Together, cost-to-serve can push past 20 percent of revenue faster than leaders expect, and yet it is often the least scrutinized, least governed, and least improved part of the business. Teams debate marketing budgets at the second decimal place while millions in operational expenses sit unanalyzed.

This is one of the most persistent root causes of the Growth Gap. Leaders treat fulfillment and CX as cost centers to be minimized instead of growth levers to be optimized.

The Blind Spot: Wholesale DNA Running a Retail Engine

Most midmarket consumer brands grew up in wholesale. Their operations teams were built to manage pallets, cases, routing guides, and replenishment flow rather than individual consumer orders. When eCommerce entered the equation, the company plugged it into the existing warehouse and process and hoped for the best.

The consequences compound quickly:

- Shipping rates are outdated or poorly negotiated.
- Pick and pack is inefficient.
- Packaging is not appropriately sized.
- Split shipments become normal.
- Returns routing is slow or inconsistent.
- Customer service lacks context, training, or empowerment.
- No one owns cost-to-serve as a growth variable.
- No one turns return reasons into action.
- No one asks whether fulfillment performance is suppressing conversion or LTV.

This is how brands end up flying blind: One of the largest levers in the P&L is completely disconnected from the teams responsible for growth. When freight, fulfillment, and returns are treated as unavoidable overhead rather than controllable variables, eCommerce becomes more costly than it needs to be and less profitable than it could be.

What Cost-to-Serve Breaks Downstream

When operational fundamentals are subpar, there are three ways the business will suffer immediately:

1. **Profitability compresses quietly and consistently.** You cannot scale profitability when a significant portion of revenue disappears into waste. Unlike media spending, operations waste rarely shows up in dashboards. It accumulates silently until someone finally asks why the contribution margin never scales.
2. **CX becomes an LTV problem masquerading as a marketing problem.** The modern consumer expects fast shipping, accurate orders, easy returns, clear communication, and responsive support. When fulfillment and CX fall short, customers forgive you once, maybe twice. Then they defect quietly. Many brands assume retention is a CRM problem, a segmentation problem, or a content problem. Often, retention is an operations issue. If you ship slowly, customers stop buying. If you mis-pick, customers churn. If packaging arrives damaged or returns are painful, the repeat rate collapses. CX is not an add-on. It's the backbone of lifetime value.
3. **Ownership fades into a gray zone.** Operational issues often fall into the space where nobody takes responsibility. The operations team says eCommerce is just another channel. The marketing team assumes the operations team has it handled. The finance team sees shipping costs but doesn't know how to influence them.

This is how companies become reluctant to touch the warehouse. The fear of disruption outweighs the pain of inefficiency, so nothing changes. Meanwhile, cost-to-serve continues to climb.

Returns: The Silent Margin Killer and the Richest Insight Loop

Most brands know their return rate. Few understand it. Even fewer use it. The return rate should be used to answer questions like the following:

- Why are customers returning?

- Are certain products responsible?
- Are promotions attracting the wrong customers?
- Are product detail pages misleading or incomplete?
- Are sizes inconsistent or confusing?
- Are certain channels driving low-quality traffic?
- Are customers surprised by materials, fit, or performance?

Returns are one of the richest insight loops in eCommerce. They reveal product issues, content issues, merchandising issues, fulfillment issues, and expectation gaps. And still, many brands treat returns as an accounting line item instead of a strategic signal.

As a result, they leave the contribution margin on the table and keep spending more to acquire new disappointed customers.

What Changes When You Fix Cost-to-Serve

When brands treat fulfillment, operations, and CX as strategic levers, the system's dynamic shifts quickly.

Lower cost-to-serve creates more room for growth. Every dollar saved below the contribution line is a dollar you can reinvest above it. Lower shipping rates give you more acquisition budget. Fewer returns increase the contribution margin. Higher pick accuracy improves CX and LTV. Better packaging reduces product damage and costs.

When return reasons are identified, analyzed, and addressed, retention improves. Conversion improves, inventory efficiency improves, and margin improves. The customer gets a better experience, and the brand captures repeat value.

The operations team becomes a core input to strategy. Return data inform product development. Shipping performance informs conversion optimization. Customer service sentiment informs lifecycle messaging.

The system gets smarter and closer to the consumer, and the compounding effect is enormous.

Once the business sees cost-to-serve as a controllable growth variable, a new question emerges: Even if we know what to fix, can we change anything quickly enough to matter?

At this point, the tech stack enters the equation.

2. The Tech-Stack Trap

Just as operational constraints determine the physical limits of scale, the tech stack determines the speed and flexibility of the business. Technology should amplify strategy and enable iteration. Instead, in many brands, it subtly (and sometimes not-so-subtly) dictates what is possible, what is delayed, and what never even gets attempted.

When the stack is misaligned, growth slows for reasons that have nothing to do with demand and everything to do with architecture.

When Technology Dictates the Business, Performance Dies

If cost-to-serve friction is the hidden tax, the tech stack is the speed and capability layer. And in most underperforming brands, technology is either so outdated that it *strangles* the business or so overbuilt that it *distracts* the business.

Both scenarios widen the Growth Gap for the same reason. The eCommerce business evolves to become technology-driven rather than merchant-driven.

Most brands develop their tech stack organically rather than intentionally. They accumulate tools, plug-ins, customizations, and integrations over years of reacting to symptoms instead of solving root causes. Eventually, the stack becomes slow and rigid or overwhelming and expensive.

Teams don't realize the damage until speed collapses, testing dies, and growth stalls as a result.

The bottom line is that technology should be an eCommerce enabler, but in many brands, it becomes either a constraint or a false savior.

Pattern 1: Outdated Systems, Tech-Constrained Brands

These brands are stuck on old, heavily customized platforms or outdated internal systems built for a different era.

In this situation, developers are required for basic updates. Merchandising and marketing lose autonomy. Simple tests take weeks. The road map becomes dominated by technical feasibility rather than commercial opportunity. Teams attempt to survive by building workarounds instead of thriving by building performance.

Every decision, insight, and action gets filtered through a single question: But can the system handle it?

Leaders often know the platform is a limitation but tell themselves a modernization project is too big, too risky, or too expensive. However, the real cost is staying trapped because a tech-constrained brand loses its most important eCommerce advantage: agility.

Pattern 2: Overbuilt Systems, Tech-Obsessed Brands

The opposite problem looks sophisticated at first. These brands have invested in enterprise-grade architecture, deep customization, and a technical stack that is unfortunately built to impress rather than perform.

The team ends up using a fraction of what it built. Every new idea becomes a technical project. New tools start to become the strategy. "If we just add this new app" becomes the default answer to every problem.

When the technology stack is overbuilt, the organization becomes tech-obsessed and distracted. Meanwhile, the fundamentals stay malnourished: positioning, merchandising, content, conversion, retention, and contribution margin.

No tool or platform can solve a strategy problem, and no new integration can replace discipline and clarity.

Consequences of a Misaligned Tech Stack

Regardless of whether the stack is outdated or overbuilt, the internal consequences are the same:

1. **Speed collapses.** Slow systems kill iteration. Every update becomes a ticket. Campaigns miss windows. Testing velocity dies. Ultimately, eCommerce loses its agility.
2. **Prioritization becomes distorted.** Tech-constrained brands prioritize what the system can handle. Tech-obsessed brands prioritize tools over fundamentals. Both lose sight of what moves revenue, margin, conversion, or LTV.
3. **Teams shift from operators to ticket managers.** High-performing teams run the business. But tech-trapped teams manage developer

queues. Initiatives become focused on projects instead of outcomes. Work becomes a backlog, not a strategy.

4. **Innovation slows or stops.** If every improvement is difficult, the team stops trying. If everything requires developers, nothing gets tested. If the stack is fragile, nobody wants to touch it.
5. **Leadership loses confidence.** Deadlines slip, and road maps fail. The stack becomes the universal excuse, then eventually, the universal frustration. When leadership loses confidence, eCommerce investment dries up, and the Growth Gap accelerates.

It's Not the Code; It's the Decision System Around the Code

Tech dysfunction originates in organizational gaps, not engineering execution.

The symptoms are again familiar. Technology decisions happen in silos. The engineering or information technology (IT) team owns platform choices. The marketing team owns the marketing technology (MarTech). The operations team owns the warehouse systems. Nobody owns the commercial engine from end to end.

Everyone shapes the technology stack, but no one governs system-level and commercial coherence.

Software thus becomes the default response when fundamentals remain unclear. New tools create the appearance of progress while structural and organizational fixes remain untouched.

Leaders eventually mistake technical complexity for sophistication. Adding new tools becomes a false proxy for progress being made. In reality, the business is unknowingly doubling down on increased fragility, lower utilization, and further systemic misalignment.

Technology and platform choices reflect the worldview behind them. That's where dysfunction originates.

What Changes When the Stack Is Fixed

When brands modernize outdated systems or simplify overbuilt ones, the shift is immediate.

Tech-constrained brands regain speed and autonomy. Merchandising and marketing stop waiting in developer queues. Tests launch in hours instead of weeks. Innovation becomes normal instead of heroic.

Tech-obsessed brands regain focus. The team uses what it already has. Meeting focus shifts from new toys to key business levers. Content, positioning, and merchandising get oxygen again. Tech becomes an enabler, not a distraction.

But even a clean, fast stack can fail if the business lacks the rhythm that turns tools into an operating system.

That is the final failure in Force 4.

3. Process Failure

Even with efficient operations and a modern stack, performance will stall if the business lacks a disciplined operating rhythm. Infrastructure enables action, but process determines whether action compounds into outcomes.

Without clear cadences, decision rights, and cross-functional alignment, the organization defaults to reaction, and business momentum becomes episodic instead of cumulative.

No Heartbeat, No Compounding

Teams are working on multiple projects simultaneously, new campaigns are launched, products are released, and dashboards are updated, yet nothing is happening in concert because there is no operating rhythm that links insights to action and action to compounded results. eCommerce has been running without a heartbeat.

Without a structure to follow, speed becomes a liability. Action is mistaken for progress. Chaos becomes par for the course. The business enters the Growth Gap one reactionary and disconnected decision at a time.

The most common pattern is a missing eCommerce Value Chain. That is, there is no operational connective tissue between strategy, planning, execution, and performance review. Teams are disjointed. Marketing sets its own goals, independent of what merchandising aims to accomplish. Merchants are making their own bets without consideration of demand realities. The operations team is left out until it is too late. The finance team either makes assumptions about what will happen or polices the situation.

Leadership gets increasingly frustrated. The eCommerce team is being most affected because the chaos is self-imposed.

An eCommerce business can't function based on improvisation.

When a company views eCommerce as "the digital execution team," it will not invest in decision rights, cadences, governance, or cross-functional alignment. Therefore, no one will be responsible for the operating rhythm. No one will protect planning. No one will ensure that the strategy connects to the execution.

Oftentimes, the organization's leaders will exacerbate this problem unknowingly. They are pushing for speed without a structure. They are rewarding fire drills. They are tolerating missed handoffs. They are treating eCommerce performance as the outcome of a collection of independent events rather than a coordinated business system.

How Process Failure Shows Up

You can see this failure long before the numbers collapse:

- There is no sales and operations planning (S&OP) process, or eCommerce is not participating appropriately.
- The weekly business rhythm is inconsistent and/or unclear.
- The business is not conducting a regular monthly cross-functional business review.
- The annual planning process is not reconciling strategic objectives and capabilities.
- The company has no road map beyond ninety days.
- The company does not have a brand calendar that eCommerce can use to align with.
- The decision rights for eCommerce are unclear, leading to politics instead of decision-making.
- The company has developed a fire-drill culture, and the fire-drill culture has become the company's operating model.
- The communication channels within the organization are fragmented, and there are multiple, conflicting versions of the truth.
- Leadership is experiencing increasing levels of frustration and decreasing confidence in forecasting.

This is how the Growth Gap expands without anyone noticing. The reason that results are unpredictable is that the operating rhythm is unpredictable.

What Happens When Rhythm Exists

When a brand installs a real operating rhythm, everything sharpens:

- On a weekly basis, the team transitions from reporting to providing insights and taking action. As a result, trends are identified earlier. Risks are mitigated. Success is repeated.
- On a monthly basis, the company reviews performance in context: headwinds, tailwinds, contribution margin, customer health, inventory dynamics, channel interactions, and the costs to serve. Patterns begin to emerge, and decisions become better informed.
- On an annual basis, strategy and finance reconcile with capability and execution. Ambition from the top meets execution from the bottom. The road map becomes intentional and not improvised.

The culture changes, too. Chaos recedes and noise dies down. Confidence increases all the way to the board level. Decision-making accelerates and stress drops. Teams can work both in the business and on the business.

At this point, your operating rhythm becomes a competitive advantage.

Why Force 4 Widens the Growth Gap

Force 4 is the substrate. When it's weak, every other force becomes more pronounced:

- A clear strategy still gets undermined by fulfillment friction.
- A clear P&L still fails to scale if returns and shipping consume the profit margin.
- A strong eCommerce leader still gets constrained by a fragile technology stack and a nonexistent cadence.

This is why some brands feel like they're doing everything right and still can't seem to reach the next milestone. They created a vision. They diagnosed the truth. They hired someone to execute. However, the machine supporting the team cannot scale to the company's needs.

When the underlying infrastructure and process are improved, the infrastructure supports the speed necessary for the business, and the operational rhythm creates the link between insight and action. The Growth Gap then shrinks without requiring heroic efforts, and growth is repeatable.

CEO BRIEFING

Force 4: The Infrastructure and Process Gap

- **Truth:** You cannot scale eCommerce on intention. You scale it on cost-to-serve, a right-sized technical stack, and an effective operating rhythm. When the machine is weak, every growth lever becomes expensive, slow, and fragile.
- **Red Flag:** If profitability refuses to scale, returns and fulfillment issues recur, basic site changes take too long, and the week is dominated by fire drills instead of decisions, this is not a marketing issue. It's an infrastructure and operating system failure.
- **Key Question:** "Do we have the physical capability and operating cadence to scale eCommerce profitably, or are hidden costs, tech friction, and process chaos quietly setting our ceiling?"

OPERATOR DIAGNOSTIC

Force 4: Are Infrastructure and Process Setting Your Ceiling?

Answer **Yes** or **No** to each question.

Cost-to-Serve and CX

1. Do you have a clear owner accountable for cost-to-serve, not just fulfillment execution?
2. Can you break down cost-to-serve into controllable components (shipping rates, pick/pack, packaging, split shipments, returns processing, support cost) and track them over time?
3. Are outbound shipping and returns treated as strategic levers, not unavoidable overhead?

4. Do you analyze return reasons regularly and turn the top drivers into specific actions across product, content, and operations?
5. Do CX issues get resolved permanently, or do the same problems keep resurfacing?
6. Do problems with retention and repeat rate trace back to service issues (shipping speed, accuracy, returns friction) in postpurchase feedback?

Tech Stack and Agility

7. Can marketing and merchandising execute routine changes without relying on developers for everything?
8. Can you launch meaningful tests quickly, not just discuss them?
9. Is your stack intentionally designed around business outcomes, not inherited or accumulated tool by tool?
10. Are you using most of what you already pay for, or does the team use a fraction of the system?
11. Does technology ever dictate prioritization, forcing the road map to follow feasibility instead of opportunity?
12. Is there a single owner or governing group responsible for how the stack performs from end to end, not just individual tools?

Operating Rhythm and Governance

13. Do you have a consistent weekly business rhythm that converts data into decisions and actions?
14. Do you run a monthly cross-functional business review that connects KPIs to contribution margin and customer health?
15. Is eCommerce integrated into S&OP and demand planning, not informed after decisions are made?
16. Do you have a twelve- to twenty-four-month road map that includes both initiatives and capability building, not just a rolling ninety-day scramble?
17. Are decision rights clear enough that decisions don't require multiple meetings and consensus loops?
18. Do campaigns, merchandising moves, and inventory realities connect through a shared calendar and planning cadence?

Predictability and Confidence

19. Does leadership trust the operating model enough to invest with confidence?

20. Does the business feel calm and predictable, or is it reactive and fragile?

Scoring and Interpretation

Yes to 16–20 questions: Your infrastructure and operating rhythm support scale. Cost-to-serve is governed, the stack enables speed, and processes create compounding execution.

Yes to 11–15 questions: Partial readiness. You can grow, but friction is setting a ceiling. The business will feel periodically constrained by operations drag, tech bottlenecks, or planning breakdowns.

Yes to 6–10 questions: Systemic constraint. Cost-to-serve, stack agility, and operating rhythm are limiting performance and distorting decision-making. Growth will remain expensive and unpredictable.

Yes to 0–5 questions: Force 4 is a primary driver of the Growth Gap. The machine cannot carry scale, and teams will keep compensating with promotions, heroics, and reactive spending.

Summary

The Infrastructure and Process Gap is the scalability failure that occurs when the machine behind eCommerce cannot support growth. Cost-to-serve inefficiencies compress margins, tech-stack dysfunction slows iteration, and process failure creates a fire-drill culture where activity replaces compounding progress. When the substrate is weak, every growth lever becomes slower, more expensive, and more fragile.

Brands cannot out-market broken plumbing. Scale requires operational capability, technical agility, and an operating rhythm that turns insight into action.

Next, we address the demand layer by examining the Demand-Generation Gap, the force that makes growth feel expensive when the brand is not earning demand and the system is not compounding it.

Case Study: The Infrastructure and Process Gap

When Speed Collapses Under the Weight of Complexity

The global furniture brand believed it had an infrastructure problem. Business performance slowed, campaigns took weeks to launch, and site changes piled up in a backlog. Reporting lagged reality. Each quarter ended with the same conclusion from the team: "We need better tools."

Over time, the tech stack and ecosystem expanded: New analytics platforms. New personalization tools. New project management software. New agencies to operate them. Each addition promised better results. Each added friction instead.

Simple changes required coordination across multiple teams and vendors. Data lived in different systems with different definitions. By the time insights reached decision-makers, the moment had passed. Testing cycles lengthened, learning decayed, and the organization responded to volatility with delay.

The problem was never technology. It was process debt.

Tools had been purchased faster than the operating discipline had been built. Decision rights were unclear. Prioritization shifted weekly. Work entered the system without sequencing or exit criteria. Infrastructure was optimized for activity rather than for learning or speed.

As pressure increased, teams stopped experimenting. The cost of change became too high. Every test felt risky. Every deployment required justification. Instead of enabling iteration, infrastructure became another monster to manage.

This business had an Infrastructure and Process Gap. It had invested in capabilities without designing the system that would enable those capabilities to work together. Infrastructure existed, but it was not aligned to a clear operating rhythm or decision cadence. Data were abundant, but insight was scarce. Speed was sacrificed in the name of control, and control was lost anyway.

CHAPTER 10

Force 5: The Demand-Generation Gap

Why Growth Gets Expensive When Demand Isn't Earned

If the Strategy Gap is about direction, the Financial Linkages Gap is about truth, the Capability and Organizational Gap is about execution, and the Infrastructure and Process Gap is about scalability, the Demand-Generation Gap is about whether the market wants what you're selling enough to make growth efficient.

This is the force that convinces teams they have an "ad problem" when they really have a demand problem.

When demand generation is healthy, acquisition feels like capture. You show up, you earn attention, you convert intent, and your retention engine compounds the value.

When demand generation is broken, growth becomes manufactured. Paid media props up demand instead of amplifying it. Promotions become your brand voice. The site works harder than it should. Retention becomes a leaky bucket you keep trying to refill. ROAS starts getting treated like a moral judgment instead of a tactical signal.

This force shows up in five failures that all point to the same reality: The brand is not earning enough demand to make eCommerce efficient, and the system downstream is not converting and compounding the demand it does earn. These five failures are as follows:

1. Brand decay and undifferentiated positioning
2. ROAS mythology and mismanaged performance marketing
3. Conversion and merchandising failures
4. The retention deficit
5. Postpurchase and voice-of-the-customer (VOC) blindness

These aren't separate problems. They're one loop. When the brand gets quiet, the business leans harder on paid media to fill the void. When performance marketing is managed by myths, the brand will pay more for today's revenue while starving future demand. When on-site conversion is weak, you pay more for the same number of sales. When retention is weak, CAC tolerance collapses. When VOC is ignored, the system never learns fast enough to fix itself.

That's the Demand-Generation Gap: demand, conversion, and retention breaking as a system.

1. Brand Decay and Undifferentiated Positioning

Demand generation starts before performance marketing. It starts with whether the brand is distinct enough to earn attention without buying it. When positioning is vague and the story is inconsistent, paid media becomes a substitute for relevance. Over time, CAC rises, conversion weakens, and promotions become the loudest thing the market hears.

It is easy to recognize brand decay in action: The brand gets quieter, and growth gets more expensive.

When the Brand Gets Quiet, Everything Gets Expensive

Consumer brands routinely think their biggest challenge is acquisition costs, competition, or the algorithm. Underneath, the real problem is often simpler.

Their brand equity is shrinking.

Brand-equity decay seldom announces itself. Revenue can look fine. A campaign can still "work." Promotions will still move inventory. But underneath, the brand is losing identity, uniqueness, and an emotional connection to consumers. The first place you feel it is eCommerce because eCommerce is the channel where nothing stands between the consumer and the brand. It's the purest reflection of the brand's strength.

Brands often don't realize they have a brand-equity problem because they don't measure the right things. They may not have the budget for formal studies of brand awareness or market share. But the signals are still there if you know where to look:

- **Declining or low repeat rates:** This is a sign that consumers don't feel a real connection.
- **Generic and fatigued creative approach:** Assets look interchangeable with those of competitors. The brand repeats messages not because they're working but because it has nothing else to say.
- **Flattening CRM and social follower growth:** Your audience is not expanding, regardless of spending.
- **Falling share of search:** This is a pure signal of shrinking brand-driven demand.
- **Low lifetime value:** This is direct reflection of low brand resonance.
- **Competitor-obsessed thinking:** The team reacts to competitors instead of understanding customers.
- **"Performance marketing is broken" narratives:** The brand is shrinking; the ads simply reveal it.
- **No brand calendar:** Channels invent their own stories because the brand team doesn't provide one.

Brand equity is not represented by a creative trophy or award. Real brand equity creates leverage in the business by lowering acquisition costs, improving conversion, raising consumer willingness to pay full price, strengthening retention, and stabilizing forecasting. When a brand wants to grow 20 percent year over year but has declining search interest and flat audience growth, its ambition is disconnected from its reality.

When fewer people care about your brand, everything downstream gets harder:

- Acquisition gets more expensive.
- LTV shrinks.
- Paid media props up demand instead of amplifying it.

- Competitors feel louder because you feel quieter.
- Every campaign feels like a grind.

The root causes are rarely "we need better creative assets." They're strategic:

1. **Lack of long-term brand narrative.** Teams operate on a season-to-season and promotion-to-promotion basis. They lack a multi-year story that says: "Here's who we are, the world we believe in, and why our products matter." Without this, everything becomes reactive and tactical.
2. **Overreliance on short-term tactics as identity.** Flash sales, bundles, new customer offers, Black Friday extensions, and so forth drive revenue but erode meaning.
3. **Vague positioning that can't answer "why us" in one sentence.** Weak positioning forces eCommerce to work too hard for every click, add-to-cart, and conversion.
4. **Weak product storytelling that describes features instead of meaning.** Brands talk in terms of categories rather than customers. They explain what the product is rather than what it does for the user.

When a brand stops telling a consistent, product-led story and starts leaning on "growth tactics" as its primary engine, brand-equity decay begins. Brand decay rapidly widens the Growth Gap by shrinking productive demand, and meanwhile, teams blame the channels.

When brand equity is healthy and strong, acquisition costs drop dramatically as organic and direct traffic demand grow. Repeat rates rise, and LTV increases. As a result, the eCommerce contribution margin expands across the board. The entire team gains confidence in the plan because the story is clearer, the positioning is tighter, and the creative approach becomes more distinct. Demand feels earned instead of manufactured or rented.

And when demand is earned, everything downstream gets easier.

2. ROAS Mythology and Mismanaged Performance Marketing

When brands feel pressure, they reach for the most visible lever: paid media. And when paid media becomes the primary growth engine, the organization starts worshipping the easiest number to track. ROAS thus becomes a proxy for discipline, a proxy for profitability, and eventually a proxy for strategy.

The problem, of course, is that ROAS is a media metric, not a business model. Without economic guardrails, it distorts decisions, reallocates spending incorrectly, and weakens demand over time.

When a Tactical Metric Becomes the Strategy, Growth Gets Distorted

As brand decay shrinks the pool of people who care, performance marketing myths distort how teams choose to reach them. Few topics create more confusion inside eCommerce brands than ROAS. Entire budgets, agency relationships, and strategic decisions hinge on a metric most companies misuse.

The myth is simple and destructive: ROAS is the primary performance KPI.

The reality is uncomfortable: ROAS is a tactical signal at best, and at worst, it's just noise.

Brands will set arbitrary ROAS targets based on finance input, prior performance data, or ego. More often than not, these targets have little to do with contribution margins, break-even economics, or lifetime value. Therefore, teams are optimizing for a KPI versus optimizing for their business.

ROAS mythology is one of the fastest and most damaging ways brands widen the Growth Gap.

Performance metrics such as ROAS tell us about the efficiency of media. Business metrics, however, such as the contribution margin, the CAC:LTV ratio, and the percentage of net revenue generated through performance marketing, provide insight into the sustainability of the brand's growth. When ROAS is used as the "North Star," teams make incorrect decisions, track incorrect metrics, and incentivize the incorrect behaviors.

Here are four common missteps that occur as a result of ROAS mythology:

1. **Arbitrary ROAS targets disconnected from the P&L.** Finance or leadership sets a "minimum acceptable ROAS" without linking it to the contribution margin or variable cost logic. A decision that should be based on a financial calculation becomes a matter of personal opinion.
2. **Treating performance marketing as a fixed cost.** Your team has a set budget for performance marketing at the beginning of each year, and once allocated, it remains constant, similar to your overhead expense. In actuality, performance marketing is a variable leverage that should either grow or shrink, depending on its performance.
3. **Overvaluing last-click attribution.** Most brands do not measure LTV, or if they do, they do not relate LTV to CAC, so last click is the standard. This creates a large underweighting of introducer and influencer channels.
4. **Overanalyzing individual channels.** Rather than analyzing the overall system, teams obsess over ROAS per channel. However, different channels perform different roles: Some channels serve as an introduction, others serve as influencers, and others convert. It is unreasonable to expect each channel to meet the same ROAS requirements. It would be equivalent to demanding that each player on a basketball team be able to rebound, pass, and shoot equally well.

Ultimately, ROAS mythology distorts reality to the point where prospecting is neglected, retargeting is overfunded, and promotions become the means of maximizing efficiency. The brand gets weaker over time instead of stronger.

There are several common symptoms of ROAS myths in action in a business:

- Channel-by-channel performance policing: Each platform is judged independently instead of managing the blended system.
- Turning off prospecting during tough months: The brand stops planting seeds when it most needs new customers.

- Overreliance on retargeting: The brand pays repeatedly to convert the same shrinking pool of people.
- Finance versus marketing arguments: Finance wants higher ROAS. Marketing wants more budget. Both parties are misguided if their goals are not aligned with the contribution margin.
- Agencies constrained by artificial rules: Internal teams give agencies ROAS targets instead of business goals.
- Incorrect budgeting logic: Performance marketing is treated as a static line item instead of a variable investment tied to payback.
- Misreading creative performance: Weak creative performance gets blamed on "platform changes" rather than a lack of story or variation.
- Overusing discounts: While promotions artificially inflate ROAS on paper, they also decrease profit margins.
- No LTV:CAC ratio logic: Teams can't articulate what they're willing to spend to acquire a customer.
- Growth stalls despite high ROAS: This occurs because ROAS can be high even when a brand is shrinking.

When a brand stops worshipping ROAS and starts managing performance marketing as part of a business system, everything sharpens.

Teams establish ROAS floors based on the break-even contribution margin. Getting close to the floor isn't scary; it's healthy. However, spending to a point below the ROAS floor is unacceptable unless there is a strategic justification for accepting lower levels. The marketing and finance teams work together to develop a unified approach to performance marketing.

Brands move away from fixed budgets and toward variable spending. Instead of asking, "How much money do I have to spend?" teams ask, "What level of profitable demand can I generate this quarter?"

Brands establish goals for the following:

- Percentage of net revenue generated through performance marketing
- Percentage of net revenue expended on performance marketing
- Acceptable CAC compared to LTV

A brand can have high ROAS and still be contracting. This is the trap. ROAS can appear excellent even while demand generation declines because it is easier to demonstrate excellent ROAS when you are harvesting existing consumer intent versus generating new intent.

Correcting ROAS mythology issues does not require eliminating or rejecting ROAS outright. It simply necessitates reducing its overall importance in the conversation by doing the following:

- Establish ROAS floors tied to your break-even contribution margin.
- Manage your spending as a variable lever, not as a fixed budget.
- Utilize CAC and LTV as strategic guardrails.
- Analyze performance as a blended system, not as a channel-by-channel judgment.

Performance marketing is then incorporated into the ecosystem rather than driving it. It is neither a magic bullet nor a scapegoat. It is not the driving force behind your business but instead a measurement signal within a highly functioning system.

Said another way, ROAS is not the engine. It is a gauge.

3. Conversion and Merchandising Failures

Even when a brand earns attention and buys traffic efficiently, the system can still fail at the moment of truth: conversion. Underperforming brands often assume conversion is a design issue, but the biggest leakage usually comes from unclear ownership, weak merchandising discipline, and a site experience that was never built to sell. When the site cannot translate intent into orders, every growth input becomes more expensive, and every ROAS conversation becomes more fragile.

When the Site Can't Sell, Paid Media Can't Save You

Many brands believe that conversion issues must result from poor website design.

"Let's change the product detail page (PDP) layout," "We should make the call-to-action (CTA) buttons bigger," and "Pick a new hero image and do an A/B test!" are all common statements in the halls of eCommerce brands.

However, the most impactful conversion failures are not technical or design oriented. They're organizational. Examples include the following:

- PDPs are developed by committee rather than developed specifically to help drive conversions.
- Navigation is built on internal logic instead of customer logic.
- Generic product merchandising doesn't surface heroes and bestsellers.
- Brand teams make commerce-related decisions too far down the sales funnel.
- No experimentation culture exists because the company's systems are not set up for testing.

In high-performing organizations, there is a very clear hierarchy when it comes to the different areas of their websites:

- The home page is a brand moment.
- PLPs and category pages are shared between the brand and eCommerce.
- PDPs tend to be heavily influenced by the eCommerce side.
- Cart and checkout belong to eCommerce.

When this gets violated, conversion collapses quietly:

- Add-to-cart stalls.
- The attach rate stays low.
- AOV stagnates.
- Dollars spent per visit stay weak.
- Paid media looks worse than it really is because the site can't convert intent efficiently.

Converting your customers has one of the largest and fastest impacts on demand generation because converting incremental visitors increases the contribution margin generated by the same amount of traffic. It also helps reduce psychological dependence on ROAS debates, because the website begins to do its job.

4. The Retention Deficit

Demand generation is not just about acquiring customers. You must also keep them. With continually rising CACs, retention is the safeguard and compounding layer that ensures acquisition is an asset instead of a treadmill. When repeat-purchase behavior is weak, the brand is forced to reacquire customers (and revenue) every month through paid media, promotions, and constant reacquisition.

When Customers Don't Come Back, Acquisition Becomes a Treadmill

Many brands fixate on acquisition while ignoring their retention deficit, often a severe one.

Historically, brands with wholesale DNA have been trained to think in terms of selling to retailers (sell-in) and having them sell through to the consumer. Retailers were responsible for building relationships with those consumers. However, with the advent of eCommerce, the dynamics of the relationship changed, and now retention is something that is measurable, influenceable, and essential for the brand itself.

Signs that retention is weak include the following:

- LTV stays flat.
- CAC tolerance collapses.
- Promotions become the primary way to maintain repeat business.
- The contribution margin shrinks.
- Forecasting becomes volatile.
- The business must replace huge portions of last year's customers just to stay flat.

The reasons for retention deficits among brands are consistent:

- There is no dedicated owner of retention.
- Benchmarks and goals for retention do not exist.
- Segmentation of customers is poor.
- A lifecycle strategy for customers is nonexistent.

- Promotions train the customer.
- The postpurchase experience is transactional instead of reinforcing value.

Be careful not to misconstrue retention as a nice-to-have. In a direct-to-consumer retail channel like eCommerce, retention is the economic lever that enhances a brand's acquisition capability.

In other words, without strong retention, acquisition is a treadmill, and with strong retention, acquisition compounds.

5. Postpurchase and VOC Blindness

Postpurchase experience is where demand either compounds or leaks. If customers are disappointed, confused, or unsupported after the sale, they do not come back, and they rarely tell you directly in a way the organization can act on. Meanwhile, the business keeps spending to acquire new customers without learning why previous ones churned.

A healthy demand system requires a continuous VOC loop that feeds product, merchandising, marketing, and CX with real evidence and actionable insights.

When the Customer's Reality Never Reaches the Organization

If retention is the engine, postpurchase experience and VOC are the fuel injectors.

Most brands obsess over the front end of the funnel and view every aspect of the customer experience after the sale as an operational requirement. The old wholesale mentality lingers. Retailers used to own returns, service, education, and loyalty. When brands continue to behave as if the customer journey ends at checkout, the costs are enormous:

- Weak onboarding and educational experiences result in customers getting little to no value out of their purchases quickly.
- Customer experience is optimized for closing tickets and calls, not creating loyalty.
- Return reasons and complaints get buried, not surfaced.
- Reviews get collected but are not analyzed for insights.

- Product and creative decisions happen without the customer's voice.
- The organization guesses what customers want, then debates, then repeats the same mistakes.

VOC blindness doesn't just harm loyalty. It blocks improvement across the entire growth system. It's why brands keep paying to reacquire disappointed customers instead of fixing the reasons they left.

When VOC becomes a constant input, the brand stops guessing and starts learning. That learning compounds into better products, better storytelling, better merchandising, better CX, and stronger retention.

Why Force 5 Widens the Growth Gap

This force is where growth becomes expensive:

- Weak brand equity leads to less demand and higher CAC.
- ROAS mythology misallocates spending and starves prospecting.
- Weak conversion forces the brand to pay more for the same revenue.
- Weak retention collapses CAC tolerance and makes growth fragile.
- VOC blindness prevents the organization from learning fast enough to get ahead.

That is the Demand-Generation Gap: the entire demand system failing to earn, convert, and compound attention profitably.

CEO BRIEFING

Force 5: The Demand-Generation Gap

- **Truth:** Growth gets expensive when demand isn't earned. Brands blame platforms and CAC, but the real constraint is shrinking brand-driven demand, mismanaged performance marketing, weak on-site conversion, and retention that fails to compound.
- **Red Flag:** If ROAS looks "fine" but growth is flat, if promotions are doing the heavy lifting, if the website is busy but not converting, and if repeat behavior is weak, you do not have an ad problem. You have a demand system problem.

- **Key Question:** "Are we earning demand and compounding it through conversion and retention, or are we manufacturing revenue through paid media and promotions because the brand and customer system isn't strong enough?"

OPERATOR DIAGNOSTIC

Force 5: Is Your Demand Engine Earned or Manufactured?

Answer **Yes** or **No** to each question.

Brand Demand and Positioning

1. Does the brand lack a clear, one-sentence "why us" that employees and customers can repeat?
2. Is share of search, organic/direct traffic, or audience growth flat relative to your growth ambition?
3. Do campaigns increasingly feel harder, more expensive, or less effective even when execution is strong?
4. Are promotions functioning as your primary "story" instead of amplification of a bigger narrative?

Performance Marketing and ROAS Discipline

5. Is ROAS treated as the primary KPI rather than a tactical signal inside economic guardrails?
6. Are ROAS targets not explicitly tied to the break-even contribution margin and CAC:LTV ratio logic?
7. Do you evaluate channels independently instead of managing blended performance and channel roles?
8. Do you cut prospecting when ROAS drops, even if the business needs future demand?

Conversion and Merchandising

9. Are PDPs controlled by brand or consensus rather than built to sell and tested continuously?
10. Is navigation, category structure, or merchandising built around internal logic instead of how customers shop?
11. Do you lack a consistent experimentation rhythm that produces weekly learning and measurable lift?

12. Does the site feel inconsistent from home page to PDP to checkout, with the funnel weakening deeper down?

Retention and Compounding

13. Do you lack a clear owner for retention, repeat rate, and LTV performance?
14. Is the CRM contribution to revenue stagnant, and are segmentation or lifecycle journeys underdeveloped?
15. Are promotions driving a disproportionate share of second and third purchases?
16. Is LTV not used to set CAC expectations and acquisition guardrails?

Postpurchase and VOC

17. Are postpurchase flows thin, generic, or mostly transactional?
18. Are returns, reviews, complaints, and VOC not reviewed on a cadence that drives action across product, brand, and CX?
19. Is CX measured primarily on efficiency instead of loyalty creation and quality of resolution?
20. Does the organization routinely make product or creative decisions without direct customer evidence?

Scoring and Interpretation

Yes to 16–20 questions: Your demand system is healthy. Demand is earned, conversion and retention compound it, and performance marketing amplifies instead of props up.

Yes to 11–15 questions: Partial strength. You have demand, but leakage in conversion, retention, or ROAS discipline is making growth more expensive than it should be.

Yes to 6–10 questions: Systemic inefficiency. The business is manufacturing revenue through tactics because the demand engine is not compounding.

Yes to 0–5 questions: Force 5 is a primary driver of the Growth Gap. Growth will remain fragile and expensive until the brand earns demand and the system compounds it.

Summary

The Demand-Generation Gap is the breakdown of the demand system, where the brand is not earning enough attention to make growth efficient, and the downstream engine is not converting and compounding what demand does exist. Brand decay, ROAS mythology, weak conversion, retention deficits, and VOC blindness form a loop that forces the business to manufacture revenue through paid media and promotions.

When demand is not earned and compounded, growth becomes expensive, volatile, and increasingly dependent on tactics that weaken the brand over time.

Next, in part 3, we shift from diagnosis to solution by introducing the eCommerce Value-Creation System, the operating framework that replaces fragmentation with structure and provides a path to close the Growth Gap.

Case Study: The Demand-Generation Gap

When Growth Is Rented Instead of Earned

At first glance, the outdoor apparel brand appeared to be growing. Revenue was up year over year. Paid media performance looked strong, the website converted reasonably well, and all dashboards showed progress.

But under the surface, something was breaking.

CACs climbed steadily and retention softened. Organic traffic flattened and promotions became more frequent. Each month required more spending to produce the same result. Growth existed, but it did not compound.

Demand was being purchased, not generated.

The organization treated demand as a faucet. When revenue dipped, marketing spending increased. When margins tightened, prospecting was cut. Performance marketing became the primary lever for hitting the number, whereas brand, storytelling, and retention were treated as secondary concerns.

Over time, the system hollowed out. New customer quality declined. LTV stagnated. The business relied increasingly on discounting to convert traffic that had little attachment to the brand. Paid channels almost exclusively captured existing demand rather than creating future demand.

This brand had a serious Demand-Generation Gap.

The failure was not in media execution. It was in treating acquisition, conversion, and retention as separate activities rather than as a loop. As pressure rose, leadership doubled down on short-term efficiency metrics. ROAS targets tightened, and prospecting budgets were cut. The business borrowed results from the future to protect the present, and each cycle made the next one harder.

PART 3

HOW TO CLOSE THE GROWTH GAP

The Road Map, Systems, and Behaviors Required to Unlock a Brand's Full eCommerce Potential

From Diagnosis to Design

How Healthy eCommerce Systems Actually Work

By the end of part 2, you hopefully feel a new kind of clarity.

Ideally, you understand why effort has not translated into repeatable growth, why smart teams keep circling the same problems, why fixes that "worked once" never seem to hold, and why eCommerce performance feels fragile even when the business appears busy and well resourced.

The Five Forces describe five interconnected ways the machine can fail:

- The Strategy Gap breaks direction.
- The Finance Gap breaks truth.
- The Capability and Organizational Gap breaks ownership.
- The Infrastructure and Process Gap breaks speed.
- The Demand-Generation Gap breaks compounding growth.

In each of these areas, the breakdown damages a different component of the same overall system. Therefore, repairing each area separately will never provide lasting results.

This is the moment where our diagnosis must give way to designing a path forward.

Part 3 will help guide your business to move beyond random tactics and trial-and-error approaches to instead construct a cohesive eCommerce operating system with a virtuous cycle: Strategy drives execution, execution generates insight, and insight refines strategy. Value creation becomes measurable and repeatable.

The following section is where the eCommerce Value Chain arrives as a foundational operating model supporting the overall eCommerce Value-Creation System.

Up to this point, we have explained why performance breaks. In part 3, we show how performance is produced when the system is healthy by zooming out and examining the entire operating system. We explore how inputs move through the business. We determine where ownership lives and how decisions are made. We analyze how demand is earned, converted, and compounded. And finally, we ensure insights flow back into planning rather than dying in dashboards.

The goal is to peel back the curtain on how high-performing eCommerce businesses operate: calmly, repeatedly, and without constant heroics. The model is designed to be attainable and practical, not uselessly aspirational.

If parts 1 and 2 helped you see what is wrong, part 3 exists to answer a harder and more important question: "What does 'good' actually look like, end to end, when this works?"

CHAPTER 11

The eCommerce Value-Creation System

The Operating Model That Resolves the Five Forces

At this point in our journey, the pattern should be unmistakable. The majority of eCommerce businesses experiencing a Growth Gap are not suffering because of weak tactics, poor execution, or lack of effort but because there isn't a coherent system in place to define strategy and translate it into repeatable outcomes.

That is exactly what the Five Forces identify, and it is also why most brands get stuck.

Each force illustrates a unique manner in which performance fails. Not at random, or episodically, but structurally.

However, none of the Five Forces occurs in a vacuum. The Growth Gap exists because the system on which the business operates is fractured, deficient, or was never intentionally designed, and thus it cannot be relied on each week to drive the brand toward the desired outcomes.

In this chapter, we will introduce the system that resolves the Growth Gap and unlocks profitable growth.

The eCommerce Value-Creation System reaches beyond a maturity model or new organizational chart to describe an operating framework for how high-performing brands run eCommerce as a complete *business* and convert potential into repeatable bottom-line performance.

The eCommerce Value-Creation System is designed to answer a single question: "How does this business consistently turn effort into profitable growth and operational excellence?" It accomplishes this by creating a connection between five separate motions that are almost always managed in isolation in underperforming brands:

- Strategic intent
- Financial reality
- Execution ownership
- Operational speed and agility
- Customer demand and LTV

For most brands, these five separate motions are managed in five separate meetings. When these motions operate independently, the Five Forces appear. Where they operate as a system, the Growth Gap is closed.

The Architecture of the System

Because of its systemic nature, the eCommerce Value-Creation System behaves like a physical structure, as shown in the accompanying figure. A structure has a foundation, load-bearing pillars, and stabilizing beams. It has a "roof" that represents the outcome the structure exists to support.

Remove the foundation, and the structure collapses under its own weight. Remove the pillars or beams, and it warps under pressure.

An eCommerce business is no different.

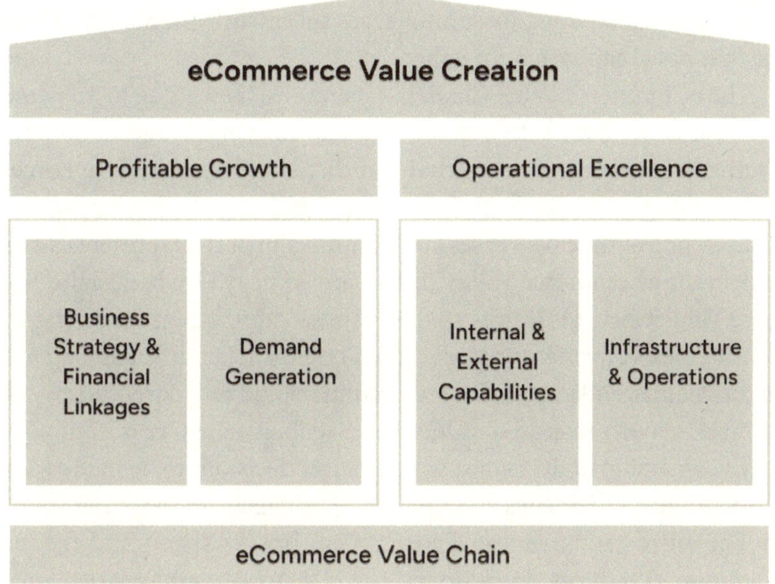

The Foundation: The eCommerce Value Chain

At the base of the system sits the eCommerce Value Chain.

This is not a simple process map taped to a wall that everyone ignores. This foundational rhythm ties the whole organization together in the pursuit of eCommerce Value Creation, defining its repeatable approach to how strategy becomes action, how action becomes insight, and how insight feeds back into better decisions.

As an operating rhythm, the eCommerce Value Chain has a robust cadence in the form of weekly execution, monthly review, and quarterly planning. The cadence has feedback loops that transform data into insights and then into actionable explanations for why things happened and what should happen next.

When the eCommerce Value Chain is working properly, the noise disappears from the system. Decisions become more straightforward, friction within teams decreases, and as a result, outcomes become more predictable.

When there is no eCommerce Value Chain, every other element of the eCommerce Value-Creation System begins to wobble as well. Even strong brands and talented teams cannot scale successfully because there is no glue that holds the system together.

The eCommerce Value Chain is *not* another "new thing to implement." Rather, it is the connective tissue that allows everything else to operate effectively. It becomes the mechanism that eliminates the Five Forces by replacing fragmentation with flow.

Each one of the Five Forces you examined in part 2 represents a critical break in the eCommerce Value Chain. The Strategy Gap breaks the eCommerce Value Chain at the top, so the business cannot translate strategy into specific roles, priorities, or trade-offs. The Financial Linkages Gap breaks the constraints, and economics are misunderstood or ignored, so execution optimizes activity instead of value. The Capability and Organizational Gap breaks ownership of decisions, which causes decisions to be made without accountability and creates an opportunity for agencies to fill the void.

The Infrastructure and Process Gap breaks speed and feedback. Therefore, execution slows down, the cost-to-serve increases, and the effectiveness of the business's most important learning cycles is diminished. The Demand-Generation Gap breaks compounding, and the business will produce expensive revenue rather than generating profitable demand.

The Five Forces do not represent five different problems. They represent five consistent and fatal ways the machine fails when the eCommerce Value-Creation System lacks an operational foundation to tie it all together.

In a healthy eCommerce Value-Creation System, the business behaves differently. It does not operate "louder." It does not operate "busier." The business operates more deliberately.

Strategy defines the role of eCommerce within the business, and financial guardrails define what growth must achieve and what it cannot compromise. Ownership ensures decisions are made close to the work and enforced consistently. Infrastructure supports speed without constraining it. Demand is earned, converted, and compounded across the full lifecycle of the customer.

Most importantly, the eCommerce Value-Creation System makes performance visible to leadership and teams.

Leadership can see where value is being created and where value is leaking. Teams know why priorities are set and not simply what they are. Road maps become stable. Forecasts gain credibility. Debate transitions from opinion to diagnosis and action.

The system delivers performance through intentional design rather than individual heroics.

The eCommerce Value Chain. Five sequential functions (Business Strategy & Voice of Consumer, Business & Product Planning, Go to Market, Execution & Customer Experience, and the Data → Insight → Action → Outcome Loop) form the operating rhythm that connects strategy to execution and execution to learning. The eCommerce Value Chain is the foundation of the eCommerce Value-Creation System. When it functions as designed, strategy becomes action, action becomes insight, and insight compounds into durable performance.

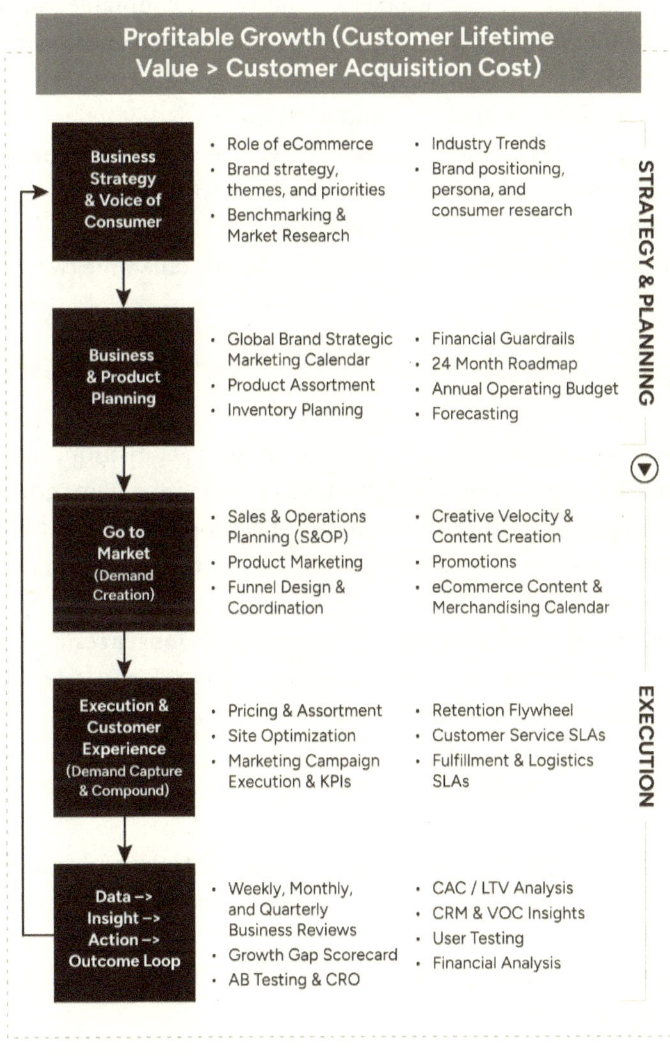

The Four Pillars

Above the foundation sit four structural pillars. Each one addresses a failure mode described in part 2. Together, these four pillars support the overall structure of the system.

1. Strategy and Financial Linkages

This first pillar creates alignment between strategic ambitions and financial realities. This pillar defines what eCommerce is accountable for, how success will be measured, and the financial constraints and enablers that shape eCommerce's ability to grow. Additionally, this pillar establishes the link between top-down goal setting and bottom-up mathematical analysis so that the organization understands both what it wants to accomplish and what it will take to accomplish those objectives profitably.

Without this pillar, strategy becomes nothing more than a narrative, and finance is reduced to enforcement. With this pillar, the two operate as one reinforcing system.

2. Demand Generation

This second pillar links brand equity, customer acquisition, conversion, and retention into a powerful engine that generates demand, captures it, and compounds future demand. In other words, this pillar creates an integrated system designed to drive top-line growth rather than creating multiple disconnected tactics fighting for budget and attention.

Thus, brand development and eCommerce no longer compete, conversion no longer compensates for lackluster demand, and retention is no longer an afterthought. The system works together as a whole.

3. Internal and External Capabilities

The third pillar ensures the appropriate level of expertise, leadership, and bandwidth to execute the right work at the right time. This pillar determines who performs which functions, how decisions are made across internal roles and external agencies, and how insights and information flow throughout the business.

In essence, this pillar represents the difference between just having people versus having true capability.

4. Infrastructure and Operations

The fourth pillar enables the system to operate quickly, accurately, and at scale. This pillar encompasses the technology stack supporting eCommerce, the mechanisms for order fulfillment, the quality of the customer experience, the reliability of eCommerce data, and the operational processes that enable the eCommerce system to operate without obstacles or friction.

If this pillar is weak, then every attempt to improve the system slows down. Conversely, when this pillar is strong, improvements compound for value creation.

None of these pillars is optional. Each one resolves a structural failure that widens the Growth Gap when left unaddressed.

The Two Beams

Resting across these pillars are two stabilizing beams. They define the outcomes the system is designed to produce.

Beam One: Profitable Growth

Supported primarily by business strategy, financial linkages, and the demand engine, this beam ensures that growth creates value rather than consumes it. In other words, revenue growth does not come at the expense of margin erosion, and investment decisions are made based on data and math, not emotion or hope.

Beam Two: Operational Excellence

Supported by capabilities and infrastructure, this beam ensures the organization can execute consistently. Speed increases, quality improves, and most importantly, customers feel the difference.

When both beams are strong, the business becomes predictable and consistent. When either one weakens, the structure flexes, and the Growth Gap will appear again.

The Roof: Value Creation

At the top of the system sits the outcome the business aims for: *value creation.*

eCommerce value creation occurs when profitable growth, operational excellence, brand strength, customer LTV, and organizational confidence reinforce one another.

Said another way, eCommerce value creation is the point at which the Growth Gap closes, eCommerce stops feeling fragile, and it *starts behaving like an asset.*

Why the eCommerce Value-Creation System Is Important

The eCommerce Value-Creation System is operational by design.

For executives, it provides clarity and a way to see how decisions connect, where risk lives, and why performance behaves the way it does. Planning becomes grounded. Forecasts become credible.

For operators, it provides focus. Priorities make sense. Work ladders up and connects logically. Insight turns into action instead of debate.

For the organization, it creates alignment. The brand, product, CX, operations, finance, and eCommerce teams stop pulling in different directions because they are working inside the same system toward the same strategic outcomes.

And for the business, it creates something rare in eCommerce: predictability. This is where high-performing eCommerce brands separate themselves.

This Is Not an Organizational Chart or a Tech Stack

The eCommerce Value-Creation System is often misunderstood because organizations look for it in the wrong places.

They look for it in head-count plans, platform ecosystem diagrams, or agency dashboards.

But none of those is the system. They are just components.

Without a governing model that defines how those components interact, adding more of them only increases complexity.

The eCommerce Value-Creation System is the logic that determines the following:

- How strategy becomes execution
- How execution becomes learning
- How learning becomes better decisions
- How decisions compound value creation over time

Put simply, tools support the system, people operate within the system, and tactics execute through the system, but the system itself is what determines whether growth is fragile or repeatable.

Making the eCommerce Value-Creation System Visible

One of the reasons that many organizations have been unable to close the Growth Gap is that the eCommerce Value-Creation System is invisible to them.

These organizations can see output metrics such as revenue, ROAS, conversion rates, and margin. However, they cannot see whether the machine producing those output metrics is improving or degrading.

Successful eCommerce organizations evaluate system health in addition to financial results.

They track whether strategy, economics, capability, infrastructure, and demand are strengthening together or pulling apart. They measure progress in quarters, not campaigns. They manage and measure eCommerce as a business system, not a tactical marketing channel. When this occurs, chaos gives way to discipline.

How Healthy Systems Behave

After you install the eCommerce Value-Creation System, your company's culture will shift from an "explanation" mindset to an "inevitability" mindset:

- From "Why did we miss our number?" to "Where is the bottleneck in the value chain?"
- From "We need better ads" to "We need a better demand engine."
- From "Who is to blame?" to "Which part of the system is failing?"

Organizational charts and new tools alone won't create this. The answer is a *system view*. Specifically, one that allows a CEO to identify exactly which lever to pull and transforms eCommerce from a mysterious black box of marketing spend and a website into a predictable engine of value creation.

Why This Chapter Matters

This chapter is the pivot point of the book.

Everything up to this point explained why performance breaks down. From here on, we discuss how performance gets built back up.

The eCommerce Value-Creation System is the framework that makes eCommerce predictable, scalable, and profitable, and it resolves the Five Forces.

Not because the team started working harder but because the machine finally started working cohesively.

In the next chapter, we move from system design to system operation, because a system is only as strong as the planning cadence that governs it.

CEO BRIEFING

- **Truth:** You cannot manage eCommerce by optimizing channels, tactics, or outputs in isolation. Sustainable growth only comes from a repeatable system that connects strategy, economics, execution, and learning.
- **Red Flag:** If performance relies on promotions, heroics, or constant road-map changes, and leadership debates results instead

of diagnosing causes, the business does not have a growth system. It has activity without compounding.

- **Key Question:** "Do we have a defined operating system for how eCommerce creates value, or are we relying on disconnected efforts and post hoc explanations for results?"

OPERATOR DIAGNOSTIC

Answer **Yes** or **No** to each question.

System Clarity

1. Can leadership clearly articulate how eCommerce creates value for the business, beyond "growing revenue"?
2. Is eCommerce understood internally as a business system, not a marketing channel or digital team?
3. Do the brand, product, finance, operations, and eCommerce teams share a common mental model for how growth is produced?

The eCommerce Value Chain

4. Do you have a defined operating rhythm that connects strategy, execution, performance review, and course correction?
5. Are weekly, monthly, and quarterly cadences consistent and protected, not overridden by fire drills?
6. Do data reliably flow from execution to insight to action, or do data stall in reporting?

Strategy and Economics

7. Are strategic goals explicitly tied to contribution margin, CAC tolerance, and LTV expectations?
8. Do teams understand which trade-offs have already been decided and which ones are still open?
9. Is eCommerce strategy stable enough to guide sequencing, not renegotiated every quarter?

Demand as a System

10. Are brand, acquisition, conversion, and retention managed as one demand engine rather than separate functions?

11. Is performance marketing governed by economic guardrails instead of arbitrary ROAS targets?
12. Does the site consistently convert intent efficiently, or is paid media compensating for weak merchandising and UX?

Capability and Ownership

13. Are roles, decision rights, and ownership clear across internal teams and external partners?
14. Is there a single accountable leader responsible for end-to-end eCommerce system performance?
15. Does the organization have the capability and bandwidth to execute the road map it has committed to?

Infrastructure and Speed

16. Does your tech stack enable fast iteration, testing, and learning rather than slowing it down?
17. Are fulfillment, CX, and operations treated as growth levers, not just cost centers?
18. Can the business absorb growth without margin leakage or operational strain?

Governance and Learning

19. Are initiatives prioritized based on system impact rather than urgency or internal politics?
20. Does leadership review eCommerce performance through a system lens, not just channel outputs?

Scoring and Interpretation

Yes to 16–20 questions: The system is largely in place. Focus on refinement, discipline, and compounding gains.

Yes to 11–15 questions: Partial system maturity. Growth is possible, but friction and misalignment are setting a ceiling.

Yes to 6–10 questions: Systemic fragmentation. Effort is high, outcomes are fragile, and the Growth Gap will persist.

Yes to 0–5 questions: eCommerce is operating tactically without a governing system. Results will remain volatile regardless of spending or talent.

Summary

The eCommerce Value-Creation System replaces fragmentation with structure and a foundation of rhythm and governance. Four pillars that resolve root causes. Two stabilizing beams that deliver profitable growth and operational excellence. And a clear outcome where value is created and compounds.

When the system functions as a whole, eCommerce becomes scalable, predictable, and durable.

But the system is only as strong as its planning discipline. Next, we build the strategic planning and annual operating cycle that turns ambition into a clear, financially grounded plan the organization can consistently execute.

CHAPTER 12

Strategy, Economics, and Planning as One System

How Direction and Constraints Enter the Machine

By now, you've seen what happens when eCommerce is asked to "hit a number" without being given a system that can produce it. In most cases, the number gets missed. That failure starts before creative work even begins, before media plans are developed, and before a single PDP is created.

That failure begins when strategy, finance, and planning operate independently of each other, speaking in three different languages.

Strategy speaks in terms of ambition. Finance speaks in terms of constraint. Planning tries to translate both into action, usually after the fact, when it's too late.

Then, eCommerce gets handed the messy output and is told to execute. Product and inventory levels lock in, and the entire organization wonders why conversion rates and margins aren't behaving as expected.

This chapter is about avoiding that failure.

Direction and constraints need to be put into the machine simultaneously. When they are not, the Strategy and Financial Linkages Gaps are never resolved. Instead, they reappear later in the year as weekly chaos, emergency promotional activities, and budget battles.

A plan is not a wish. It is a set of commitments that reconcile what you want with what you can do, and what the numbers will enable you to do.

The Failure Pattern: Borrowing Confidence from the Future

Most brands do not have a problem developing a strategic plan. Most brands have a problem reconciling their strategic ambitions with their financial realities. The board states that the company needs to grow. The CEO adds a layer of stretch to that goal. The finance team creates a budget, the brand team develops a calendar, the merchandising team develops an assortment, and the operations team prepares for increased volumes. Then, eCommerce finds out what the "plan" is after the fact and is expected to deliver numbers that it never helped shape.

This is how organizations unintentionally borrow confidence from the future. The plan appears to be decisive, and the slide deck appears to be aligned, but the only question that matters was never answered: Can this business produce this outcome, with these inputs, under these constraints? A bad plan is nothing more than deferred failure. When that key question is not answered during planning, it gets answered later by reality, usually by the second quarter (Q2), and often at the expense of profitable growth.

The First Task: Define the Role of eCommerce

In the eCommerce Value-Creation System, strategy and economics are not separate conversations.

Strategy sets direction. Economics set boundaries. Planning is the mechanism that forces both to become realistic. When these are separated, two common failures occur:

1. Strategy becomes nothing more than narrative. It may sound correct and viable, but it does not dictate how decisions are made.
2. Finance becomes enforcement. It shows up late to the party, says no, and gets blamed for being "anti-growth."

A healthy system prevents that by making economics part of strategy, not a reaction to it. That begins with a critical declaration leadership must make: the role of eCommerce.

What is eCommerce supposed to do? Is eCommerce intended to drive top-line revenue growth, protect profit margins, develop the customer database, support sell-through at wholesale customers, introduce new categories, increase LTV, expand internationally, or all of the above?

Without a defined role, the organization will argue about tactics because the strategy never made priorities or trade-offs. If leadership hasn't decided whether eCommerce is a growth engine (prioritizing top-line scale), a profit center (prioritizing contribution margin), or a brand temple (prioritizing storytelling and growing the customer database), everything downstream will be ambiguous at best, conflicting at worst.

Contradictory KPIs emerge, the brand calendar has no relation to merchandising reality, and paid media is treated like a lever with either too much or too little constraint. Worst of all, inventory is bought for one strategic priority but ultimately sold against a different one. Defining the role of eCommerce provides a clear anchor for the entire organization. Without a defined role, annual planning is nothing more than very time-consuming theater.

Operating Shift: Explicitly declare the primary mandate of eCommerce: growth engine, profit center, or brand temple. This mandate acts as the North Star during annual and quarterly planning for every downstream decision, from inventory depth to CAC tolerances. Stop trying to win on every metric and start winning on the one that defines your value-creation goal. Then, create a "Metrics That Matter" document. If the role is profit center, for example, contribution margin sits at the top. If a tactical decision (e.g., an offer-heavy discount promotion) helps revenue but hurts the contribution margin, the primary mandate will automatically kill the initiative without even needing a meeting.

Direction Requires Inputs

A strategy that can't be implemented is simply a wishful aspiration. High-performing eCommerce businesses don't decide their direction in a conference room. They define their direction based on the inputs that anchor their aspirations to reality and force alignment before they begin executing. The process of healthy planning requires the organization to agree on the plan's key inputs that will drive growth and outcomes rather than focusing solely on the desired output.

The following sections highlight critical inputs to a believable eCommerce plan.

Brand Strategy, Benchmarking, and Consumer Insights

Brand strategy is more than just a clever idea for a marketing campaign. It requires a decision regarding the target audience for the brand, the values of the brand, and how the brand differentiates itself within the competitive landscape. It is also a commitment to a consistent story grounded in a defined brand persona, current consumer research, clear positioning, competitive and category benchmarking, and an understanding of category and industry trends. Without these inputs, planning discussions devolve to internal opinions, and teams debate tactics and channels without being aligned on the customer.

When the brand, category, and consumer insights are underdeveloped, eCommerce suffers the consequences first. Unrealistic targets are set for the eCommerce business, acquisition efficiency declines, conversion needs to work harder, retention softens, and the business is forced to compensate with discounting and additional spending.

High-performing eCommerce businesses accept that brand strategy is an economic imperative.

Voice of the Customer

Average brands consider VOC as secondary CX data. High-performing brands consider VOC the truth feed of the business.

Returns, reviews, complaints, surveys, and user testing reveal to the business what matters to the customer, what erodes customer trust, what causes friction between the customer and the business, and which assumptions are incorrect. If these signals do not emerge during the planning process, the plan is developed based on internal perceptions rather than the customer's actual experiences.

When VOC is absent from planning and decision-making, you are running an internal-obsessed business instead of a customer-obsessed business.

The Global Brand Strategic Marketing Calendar

Perhaps one of the least understood planning inputs is the global brand strategic marketing calendar.

A simple campaign schedule is not enough. You need a declaration of brand themes, narratives, and priorities over time, which tells the business what stories will be told, when emphasis will shift, and where focus will be sustained.

When this calendar exists and is respected, product planning, inventory buys, and demand forecasts align naturally. Conversely, if the calendar does not exist or is ignored, each channel invents its own story, the merchandising team reacts rather than plans, and the business spends the entire year trying to reconcile the messaging mismatch it accidentally created at the beginning of the year.

Product and Inventory Planning

Inventory is strategy made physical. Struggling brands plan revenue without the inventory logic to support it, or they buy inventory without the demand system required to move it profitably.

When product, inventory, and demand are not planned together, the year becomes a sequence of forced moves. An excess of inventory is commonly addressed through promotional pricing, which reduces the gross margin. Gross margin pressure drives ROAS policing, which kills prospecting investment and ultimately reduces future demand. And on. And on.

This non-virtuous cycle often starts right away in January and ends in December with the hollow promise to "plan better next year."

Contribution Margin Guardrails

This is the part most teams avoid because it is often misunderstood and forces difficult trade-offs.

The contribution margin is the governing constraint of eCommerce. It determines what you can afford, how much paid media you can run, what shipping costs and return levels you can tolerate, and whether growth will create value or erode it.

If your plan does not include explicit contribution margin guardrails, you are planning revenue in a vacuum. A healthy system defines these floors first, then uses metrics like ROAS as tactical signals inside those guardrails. Contribution margin guardrails validate and empower ambition.

> **Operating Shift:** Implement a "No Input, No Initiative" rule. For example, to propose a 20 percent growth in retention, the team must present a VOC signal (survey data showing why customers aren't returning), inventory logic (a confirmed assortment that supports the repeat purchase), and the margin floor (maximum allowable spending to reactivate those customers). If the evidence isn't provided, the initiative and outcome are not included in the plan.

Planning Is Reconciliation

High-performing organizations run annual planning as a three-phase reconciliation process, not a set of handoffs.

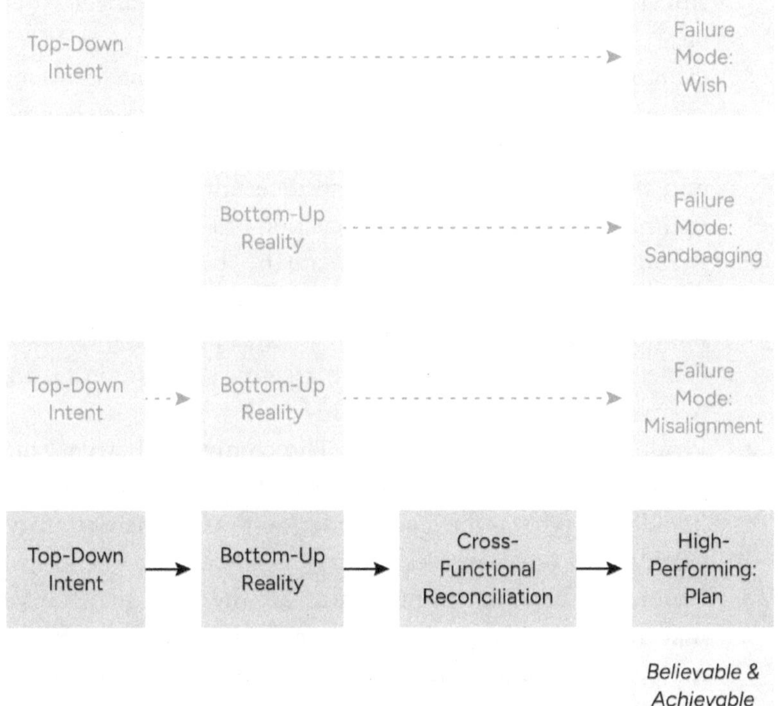

Planning as Reconciliation. Three common planning failure modes all produce plans the organization cannot commit to: Operating on top-down intent alone (a wish), bottom-up reality alone (sandbagging), or both in sequence without resolution (misalignment). The high-performing path runs top-down intent through bottom-up reality and into cross-functional reconciliation, producing a plan that is both believable and achievable.

Phase One: Top-Down Intent

This phase is led by leadership and the board and defines the direction of the company. Top-down planning is inspirational and directional, but it is not sufficient alone. The top-down plan should include details regarding the following:

- Company Goals: These goals extend beyond the P&L and address the "winning aspiration." What is the desired future state or enterprise value? How does eCommerce specifically contribute to the

EBITDA target through margin expansion or data-driven efficiencies?

- eCommerce Channel Role: This is a definitive statement on the channel's priority. Is it a growth engine (top-line focus), a profit center (contribution margin focus), or a brand temple (content and storytelling focus)? This will determine whether the team optimizes for new customer acquisition or LTV.
- Brand Narrative Priorities: These are the "big rocks" of the brand calendar. What are the three or four hero stories or brand-defining moments that must anchor the year? This prevents the Demand-Generation Gap by ensuring the marketing team isn't just reacting to seasonality but driving a narrative.
- Product and Inventory Thesis: The commercial "what" of the business. Which categories are we betting on? Which are being liquidated? What is the "good/better/best" assortment strategy for eCommerce versus wholesale?
- Nonnegotiable Constraints: These are the hard guardrails and may include fixed capital expenditure limits, specific contribution margin floors, and brand safety requirements (e.g., "We will never discount above 20 percent").

Phase Two: Bottom-Up Reality

This is where the math enters the room. This phase builds reasons to believe the top-down intent is achievable. This is also the point when fantasies die, which is why it is critical that this occurs as early as possible. This is the data-driven evidence that either validates or invalidates the top-down intent. The bottom-up plan should include details regarding the following:

- The KPI Model: The model includes historical and benchmark-backed projections for traffic, conversion, AOV, and repeat rates. If the top-down goal calls for a 20 percent increase in conversion rate without a major overhaul to the website or assortment changes, the "reality" stage will identify this as a risk.
- Demand Mix: This requires a detailed analysis of where revenue is coming from. What percentage is earned (organic/direct), owned (CRM), and paid? If growth targets require a 50 percent increase

in paid traffic while the Financial Linkages Gap mandates lower CAC, the math won't square.

- Contribution Margin by Segment: This involves evaluating the profitability of different product tiers and customer segments. Not all revenue is created equal, and this helps determine which products will need to fund the growth engine.
- CAC Tolerance Tied to LTV: This involves defining exactly how much the company can spend to acquire a customer based on their twelve-month payback. This moves the conversation from ROAS targets to unit economics.
- Paid Spend as a Percentage of Net Revenue: This establishes the "ad spend intensity" of the business. It highlights whether the brand is manufacturing revenue through expensive advertising or is earning demand through brand equity, and it should align with the defined strategic role of eCommerce.
- Operational and Capability Constraints: These are the internal limitations. Can the warehouse handle the needed volume? Are there enough resources on the team to accomplish the road map? Can the technology stack support the stated product thesis?

Phase Three: Cross-Functional Reconciliation

At this point, the plan is no longer aspirational but rather a committed course of action.

The brand, product, eCommerce, operations, and finance teams reconcile the gap between intent and reality. The output is not just a "number we must hit" but a formalized, transparent alignment on priorities, investments, constraints, and what must be true for the plan to succeed.

Without this final stage, you do not have a plan. You only have a wish with a budget attached.

Quarterly Business Reviews as the Enforcement Mechanism

Annual planning does not survive contact with reality unless it is reinforced quarterly.

Regular quarterly business reviews (QBRs) serve as an enforcement mechanism to ensure the annual plan remains relevant and coherent throughout the year. Regular QBRs are not replanning sessions. They serve as corrective actions to adjust priorities without altering core strategies.

A strong QBR revisits the original assumptions, evaluates performance against contribution margin and demand health, and adjusts priorities without rewriting core strategy. Successful QBRs foster credibility and confidence in leadership through disciplined truth-telling and a demonstrated value-chain cycle.

Operating Shift: Create a strategic gap log. During the bottom-up planning phase, the eCommerce owner must explicitly list every instance where bottom-up reality contradicts top-down intent (e.g., "Top-down requires 15 percent growth; bottom-up math shows a 5 percent ceiling based on current inventory"). Plan reconciliation cannot end until every item in the gap log is resolved by either changing the target, increasing the investment, or adjusting the strategy. You do not agree to disagree. You reconcile the math until the plan is a contract of focus.

What Changes When This Works

When strategy, economics, and planning operate as one system, the business gains a quiet confidence.

eCommerce believes in the plan. Brand calendars align with demand reality. Product and inventory stop surprising the business. The finance team stops policing because guardrails were agreed on up front.

Road maps stabilize, and outcomes compound.

This does not occur because the market suddenly got easier or the team magically got smarter but because the correct planning system was installed.

CEO BRIEFING

- **Truth:** An eCommerce plan only works when strategy and finance enter the business together. Direction without constraints becomes fantasy. Constraints without direction become policing.
- **Red Flag:** If eCommerce receives the plan late, if brand and inventory operate on separate calendars, or if ROAS targets substitute for real economic guardrails, you are planning outputs, not building a system.
- **Key Question:** "Have we reconciled ambition with bottom-up reality early enough that the plan is a commitment, not a wish?"

OPERATOR DIAGNOSTIC

Answer **Yes** or **No** to each question.

Direction and Role Clarity

1. Is the role of eCommerce clearly defined and understood by leadership?
2. Do brand, product, and channel priorities reinforce each other?
3. Are key trade-offs already decided, not renegotiated weekly?

Inputs to Planning

4. Do brand persona, consumer research, positioning, and benchmarks inform planning?
5. Does VOC actively shape decisions across brand, product, and operations?
6. Is there a global brand strategic marketing calendar guiding the year?

Product, Inventory, and Economics

7. Is inventory planned with the demand system in mind?
8. Are contribution margin targets and floors clearly defined?
9. Is CAC tolerance tied to LTV, not arbitrary ROAS targets?

Planning Discipline

10. Is bottom-up KPI analysis completed before targets are locked?
11. Does cross-functional reconciliation happen before the year begins?

12. Are quarterly reviews used to adjust execution without breaking strategy?

Scoring and Interpretation

Yes to 10–12 questions: Direction and constraints are entering the machine cleanly.

Yes to 6–9 questions: Partial integration. Expect midyear friction.

Yes to 0–5 questions: Planning is not functioning as a system.

Summary

Strategy, economics, and planning are not separate tasks. Together, they are the critical entry point of the eCommerce Value-Creation System and the first steps in the eCommerce Value Chain. When direction is clear, constraints are explicit, VOC informs decisions, and inventory planning matches the demand engine, execution becomes viable. The Strategy Gap and Financial Linkages Gap stop reappearing because the business stops guessing up front and stops scrambling later.

In the next chapter, we transition from direction and constraints to ownership, governance, and operating rhythms—because even a perfect plan is useless if nobody has the authority and process to execute it.

CHAPTER 13

Ownership, Governance, and Operating Rhythm

How the System Stays Aligned Under Pressure

Brands experiencing a Growth Gap often attempt to fix performance by redrawing their organizational chart. They hire a new VP, swap agencies, or add head count to a "stalling" channel. They rename a role and call it progress. However, an organizational chart is merely a description of reporting lines and not an operational model.

You cannot hire your way out of a systemic failure.

The Capability and Organizational Gap and the Infrastructure Process Gap rarely manifest as "we need a different organizational design." They show up as something worse. Nobody is sure who decides, so decisions are delayed or lose impact. Work stalls, and priorities get renegotiated in almost every meeting. Under pressure, the organization reverts to politics, opinions, and last-minute escalations.

This chapter is about the system components to prevent those gaps.

The eCommerce Value-Creation System does not care about titles. Instead, it prioritizes decision-making rights and operating rhythm. Without these, talent is paralyzed by ambiguity, and the business operates through heroics and fire drills rather than a repeatable cadence.

In order to close the Growth Gap, you must move from a collection of departments struggling to work together to a single cohesive system of accountability. A high-performing eCommerce business is held together by three core components: ownership, decision rights, and an operating rhythm that keeps the value chain aligned week after week, especially when the business is under pressure.

Ownership: Retiring the "Channel Manager"

The most significant difference between high-performance eCommerce businesses and struggling eCommerce businesses is the transition of the role of eCommerce leader from a "marketing manager" to a business unit owner.

In legacy models, the eCommerce lead is often viewed as a tactical coordinator whose function is to manage the website and coordinate the agencies. In the Value-Creation System, the eCommerce leader is accountable for performance across the value chain and must have governed influence on the key inputs (brand, product, finance).

If your most senior eCommerce person has accountability for the number but lacks the authority to influence the inputs that produce that number, you've hired a scapegoat instead of a business leader.

Decision Rights: Drivers and Supporters

Fragmentation happens when decision rights are trapped in "consensus culture." When everyone needs to agree, the Strategy Gap returns again, and outcomes suffer because eCommerce becomes a series of compromises.

High-performing brands use a driver/support model across the value chain. For example:

- **The Brand Story:** The brand team *drives*; eCommerce *supports* (eCommerce drives conversion execution within brand guardrails).
- **The Spend:** eCommerce *drives*; the finance team *supports* (guardrail enforcement).
- **The Product:** The product and merchandising teams *drive*; eCommerce *supports* (the product team decides what gets made; eCommerce decides how it gets merchandised and converted online).

A clear definition of ownership means knowing exactly who has the "D" (decision) and who has the "I" (input). When this is clearly defined, speed increases because the ownership boundaries that usually impede execution are dissolved.

The following sections provide some examples of common areas of frustration and the best practices for implementing a modern driver/support model.

Channel Role and Success Metrics

If eCommerce's role is ambiguous, KPIs become a debate instead of a tool. The eCommerce leader ends up defending basic priorities every quarter.

- Driver: executive leadership, with the eCommerce and finance teams as coauthors
- Support: the brand, product, IT, customer service, and operations teams
- Decision: what eCommerce is responsible for this year and what it is not responsible for

Demand and Creative Execution

This is where speed dies in most organizations. The brand team wants consistency, but eCommerce needs iteration, and agencies need fast, clear decisions.

- Driver: eCommerce drives performance, creative efforts, and conversion-led experiences.
- Support: The brand team owns the narrative, style guides, voice, and guardrails, *not* every unit and layout.
- Decision: how fast tests can ship and what "good enough" looks like for each tier of the campaign and initiative

Merchandising and On-Site Conversion

If category pages, PDP templates, and promotions are committee decisions, conversion will never improve consistently.

- Driver: eCommerce owns on-site performance and testing decisions.
- Support: The product and brand departments inform the story, hierarchy, and claims.
- Decision: what changes when the data show friction, and who has the authority to ship fixes

Pricing, Promotions, and Margin Protection

This is where the Financial Linkages Gap reappears as weekly chaos.

- Driver: The finance team owns contribution margin guardrails. The eCommerce team owns the offer strategy within those guardrails.
- Support: The brand team protects brand integrity; the operations team confirms feasibility.
- Decision: which promos run, why they run, and what they are allowed to cost

Sales and Operations Planning Integration

S&OP is where eCommerce stops being a "channel" and becomes part of the commercial system.

If eCommerce is not inside S&OP, you will plan inventory for one reality and sell it in another.

- Driver: The operations department leads S&OP.
- Support: The product, finance, eCommerce, and brand teams provide required inputs.
- Decision: inventory commitments, service levels, and demand assumptions that match the plan

The Three Rules That Make the System Work

1. The driver decides; supporters advise.
2. If it isn't in the cadence, it isn't real.
3. Escalation is a last resort, not a workflow.

Operating Shift: Create an "eCommerce Accountability & Collaboration Map" (not an organizational chart). For every core task and eCommerce experience, such as "site conversion velocity," name one team as the driver and define the support teams. If the driver for site conversion wants to test a new PDP layout, the brand team provides the brand style guardrails (support), but the brand team cannot stop the test. The driver owns the outcome, and therefore, the driver makes the final call.

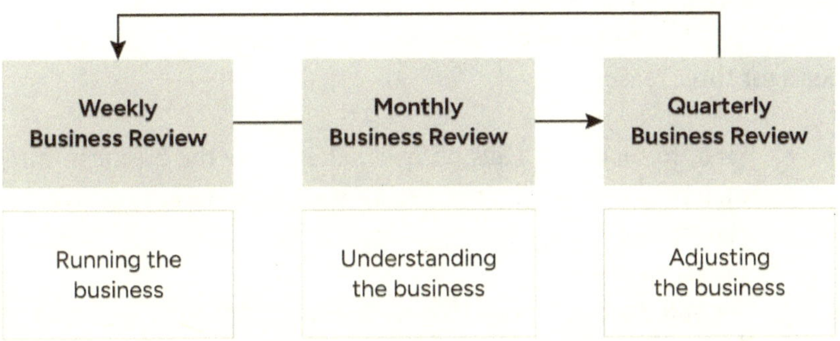

The eCommerce Operating Rhythm. Three interlocking decision forums: the Weekly Business Review, Monthly Business Review, and Quarterly Business Review. Each serves a distinct purpose: running the business, understanding the business, and adjusting the business. The cadence is self-reinforcing. Weekly execution feeds monthly learning, and monthly learning drives quarterly structural change, which drives the weekly cycle.

The Operating Rhythm: The Heartbeat of the System

A system is only as strong as the cadence that governs it. Without a fixed rhythm, the business defaults to a reactive state where urgency always trumps importance.

The eCommerce Value Chain operating rhythm consists of three distinct cycles: the weekly business review (WBR), the monthly business review (MBR), and the quarterly business review (QBR).

Weekly: Running the Business

The WBR is where the business stays out of trouble. The purpose of the weekly meeting reaches beyond simply reporting results from the previous week (a.k.a. "reading the news"). In fact, reporting is just what gets sent before the meeting so that the meeting can do its job. The weekly meeting itself is a critical diagnostic for execution. It is a performance and plan review where the team looks at key KPIs (traffic, CVR, AOV, margin) and identifies "good guys and bad guys" or "drivers and drainers." Decisions are then made to shift marketing spend, update creative assets, or address site friction in real time.

The WBR is the cornerstone of the Data → Insight → Action cycle and exists for three reasons:

- First, to make fast calls on levers that move the business immediately. For example, marketing spend, promotions, inventory exposure, site friction, customer service escalation, and fulfillment capacity.
- Second, to catch plan risks and deviations early. For example, demand softness, margin leakage, rising returns, creative asset fatigue, or supply constraints.
- Third, to assign actions with clear owners and deadlines. Not "we should," but "you will," and "by when."

If the weekly meeting concludes with agreement but there are no changes to the following week's activities, then the meeting was just group therapy.

Monthly: Understanding the Business

The MBR is about trend analysis and S&OP integration. This is where the team looks at 360-degree leading indicators (e.g., twelve-month LTV, search interest, and return rates) and where the brand, product, and eCommerce teams align on whether the demand engine is building equity or just burning cash.

The MBR is where the business stops reacting, zooms out, and starts understanding. This is where the system earns confidence. The MBR looks at contribution margin, demand mix, cohort health, LTV signals, return reasons, VOC trends, and operational performance.

The discussion must go beyond an interesting story about the month. The MBR is a decision-making event for the next month. What are we leaning into? What are we stopping? What is breaking that needs to be fixed before it compounds?

The MBR is where the finance and eCommerce teams become allies because the business is finally looking at the same reality.

Quarterly: Adjusting the Business

As discussed in chapter 12, the QBR is the "truth-telling" session. The QBR is where we reassess the road map and reallocate capital for future initiatives. If a specific initiative has failed to drive the expected results, it will be eliminated, or its focus will be changed.

This is where you protect the plan without pretending the world did not change.

There are three key activities that a good QBR should include:

- First, it revisits the original assumptions. What did we believe would be true? What is true now?
- Second, it re-anchors to constraints, such as contribution margin floors, CAC tolerance, and operational capacity.
- Third, it adjusts sequencing, not strategy. You can change the order of moves without changing the destination every quarter.

The QBR is also where the team earns trust with leadership because the team replaces unfounded optimism and "hand-waving" with transparency and consistency.

S&OP: The Missing Link

For many eCommerce brands, a key point of friction is the disconnect between the marketing and operations teams. High-performance systems integrate S&OP into the monthly rhythm. When eCommerce plans a massive "new customer" push, the operations team must be ready for the volume, and the merchandising team must ensure the "introductory" inventory is in stock. When these teams don't talk, you leave growth on the table in exchange for out-of-stock notices and customer service meltdowns. You planned inventory for one reality and marketed into another.

Operating Shift: Hard-code three recurring high-performance rituals into the company calendar:

1. The WBR: A sixty-minute diagnostic session focused on the value chain. It is a no-blame zone dedicated to identifying bottlenecks and adjusting tactical levers (spending, offers, site friction) in real time.
2. The MBR: A ninety-minute strategic alignment session.
3. A weekly S&OP meeting where eCommerce is included, every time.

How This Avoids Death by Organizational Chart

Heroic behavior ceases once an organization has put in place both governance and rhythms. In other words, the company relies less on its best people to consistently bail out the business and instead on systems or "machines" that produce consistent results. Accountability becomes transparent because the scorecard doesn't lie, and the teams gain confidence because they know exactly what they own.

When teams feel the pain of misalignment, they often reach for a reorganization because it looks decisive. But a reorg without decision rights is just a reshuffle. It moves boxes, not bottlenecks.

The fix is structural:

- Name the drivers.
- Define the calls they own.
- Put those calls into a cadence.
- Integrate eCommerce into S&OP so that the commercial plan is one plan.
- Enforce the rules when pressure hits, especially when pressure hits.

What Changes When It Works

Once the organization has established ownership and rhythms, the business feels different. Decisions get made at the right altitude. Small decisions stay closer to the source of the work. Big decisions get made with the right people, not the largest group possible.

The meeting load drops because meetings stop being the place where people negotiate legitimacy. Speed improves because teams no longer need to revisit and reargue prior discussions. The finance team stops policing. The brand team stops blocking. The eCommerce team stops improvising. The operations team stops getting surprised. As such, the system holds together, and as long as the system is operating well, performance will no longer be viewed as tenuous.

In the next chapter, we will focus further on the mechanics of the weekly engine—that is, how data turn into insight, how insight turns into action, and how action turns into outcomes, all without relying on heroics.

CEO BRIEFING

- **Truth:** You do not have an eCommerce operating system until ownership and decision rights show up as a protected cadence. Under pressure, culture follows structure.
- **Red Flag:** If weekly meetings produce agreement but not decisions, if cross-functional calls depend on escalations, and if eCommerce is not integrated into S&OP, you are running on personalities, not governance.
- **Key Question:** "When things get tight, do we get faster and clearer, or do we get louder and slower?"

OPERATOR DIAGNOSTIC

Answer **Yes** or **No** to each question.

Decision Rights

1. Do we have one clear driver for each critical workflow in the value chain, with supporters defined?
2. Do drivers have real authority to make calls without committee approval?

3. Do we have a shared rule for when the brand team's input is guardrails versus approvals?
4. Are pricing and promotional decisions governed by contribution margin guardrails, not weekly negotiation?

Operating Rhythm

5. Does the weekly forum produce decisions, owners, and deadlines, not just reporting?
6. Does the monthly forum surface system truth, contribution margin, demand mix, VOC, and operational performance?
7. Does the quarterly forum adjust sequencing without rewriting strategy or resetting priorities randomly?
8. Are annual commitments translated into a calendar that the business actually follows?

S&OP Integration

9. Is eCommerce a required input to S&OP, not an output of it?
10. Do inventory commitments reflect demand reality and marketing plans, not hope?
11. Do service levels, fulfillment capacity, and cost-to-serve assumptions show up in planning before the peak hits?

Behavior Under Pressure

12. When performance misses, do we diagnose bottlenecks in the chain rather than assigning blame?
13. Do decisions get faster when pressure rises, or do they slow down and escalate?
14. Do teams trust the cadence enough to stop creating parallel meetings and side deals?
15. Does leadership enforce the rules of the system when the loudest voices want exceptions?

Scoring and Interpretation

Yes to 12–15 questions: The system will hold under pressure. Focus on tightening and compounding.

Yes to 8–11 questions: The structure exists, but decision rights or cadence discipline will break when stress rises.

Yes to 4–7 questions: Fragmentation risk. Expect slow decisions, recurring conflict, and reactive execution.

Yes to 0–3 questions: No operating system. You are depending on heroics, and the Growth Gap will persist.

Summary

Ownership, governance, and rhythm are how the Value-Creation System stays aligned in the real world. Organizational charts do not create execution. Decision rights do. Cadence does. S&OP integration does. When those elements are installed and enforced, eCommerce stops being a cross-functional argument and becomes a business that the organization can run with speed, clarity, and confidence.

CHAPTER 14

The Demand Engine

How Brands Earn, Convert, and Compound eCommerce Demand

To close the Demand-Generation Gap, you need to shift from being a "faucet" brand, simply managing the flow of demand, to becoming a brand with a demand-generation engine.

In a high-performing eCommerce system, demand is a continuous loop where brand equity, performance media, site experience, and lifecycle marketing operate as one self-reinforcing machine. When this engine is tuned, acquisition gets cheaper, conversion improves, and retention compounds the value of every dollar spent on acquisition. Conversely, when the demand engine is nonexistent or broken, the business is simply renting customers at a price that will eventually exceed their value.

This demand engine loop lives across two core steps in the eCommerce Value Chain:

- Go-to-Market: Where demand is earned, shaped, and introduced into the system. Go-to-market includes brand storytelling, product marketing, funnel coordination, creative velocity, promotions, content, and the global eCommerce calendar.
- Execution, Operations, and Customer Experience: Where demand is converted into revenue, fulfilled, and compounded through customer LTV.

Who Owns the Demand Engine

The most common reason demand systems fail is that no one owns the loop. While functional ownership is distributed, accountability cannot be. In the Value-Creation System, the head of eCommerce must own the demand engine from end to end. They are not necessarily executing every lever, but they are accountable for the performance of the loop and how demand is earned, captured, converted, and compounded.

This requires a delicate orchestration of cross-functional interdependencies. The brand team owns the narrative consistency that creates demand, while the performance marketing team owns the media execution that captures it. The site and merchandising teams own the monetization and conversion mechanics of that traffic, and CRM and retention ensure that the value of each customer compounds over time. The operations and customer service teams own fulfillment and postpurchase trust. Finally, the finance team sets the economic guardrails that keep the engine from burning too much cash in the pursuit of vanity growth. When these functions operate in silos, the demand engine fails. When they are aligned under a single leader and loop, the engine gains compression.

> **Operating Shift:** Move from functional silos to value-chain accountability. This means the head of eCommerce must stop acting as a "channel manager" and start acting as a general manager. Instead of just reporting on what happened in the warehouse or the brand studio, they must have the authority to influence those inputs before they reach the site. This requires defining clear driver/support roles for every link in the loop. For example, while the brand team drives the aesthetic of a campaign, eCommerce must drive the commercial layout of the landing page. When you name the drivers for each intersection, you eliminate the ownership boundaries that cause demand to leak out of the engine.

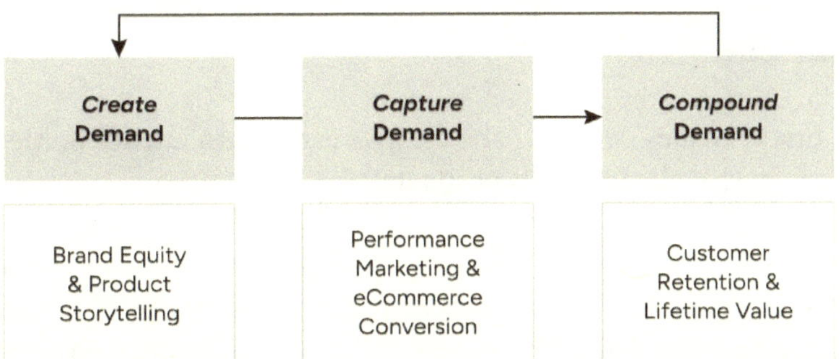

The Demand Engine. Three interconnected motions (Create Demand, Capture Demand, and Compound Demand) form a recirculating loop. Brand equity and product storytelling create demand. Performance marketing and eCommerce conversion capture it. Customer retention and lifetime value compound it back into the engine. When all three motions are managed as one system, demand gets cheaper to acquire, more predictable to convert, and more valuable over time. When they are managed in isolation or ignored, the loop breaks and the Growth Gap widens.

The Three Components of the Engine

The demand engine operates through three distinct motions. If any motion is weak, the entire engine loses compression.

1. Creating Demand (Brand and Performance Creative)

As discussed earlier in the book, brand decay is the silent killer of the demand engine. When the share of search declines and creative assets become interchangeable with those of competitors, media spend must work harder just to hold ground. In that state, demand is not being earned. It is being forced.

High-performing brands view the performance creative team as the connection point between brand vision and media execution. These brands don't just run "ads." They translate brand and product stories into clear, relevant narratives and then deliver that story to the right customer persona. There is nothing mysterious about how modern digital algorithms function. Algorithms are simply programmed to identify and reward relevance at scale. The better a brand can earn attention through storytelling, clarity, and resonance, the more the platforms will reward it with lower costs and greater scale.

The brand creates demand. The creative assets earn attention. Media is capturing what already exists upstream.

> **Operating Shift:** Replace campaign-based marketing with a regimented content loop. This requires a unified eCommerce calendar where the brand and performance teams align on three to four hero narratives per quarter. The KPIs that measure this component of the demand engine are share of search, search interest, and direct traffic. If these are declining, your brand is decaying, and no amount of media hacking will save the engine.

2. Capturing Demand (the Conversion Loop)

Once attention is earned, the system can move to capturing.

Demand capture is where the media mix and the on-site experience must reconcile. It is also where most ROAS myths finally collapse.

A healthy demand engine does not chase vanity ROAS targets. Rather, it optimizes for customer acquisition cost relative to LTV. Capturing demand is the handoff between the ad and the PDP. When traffic is driven to a site that is slow, confusing, or lacking a story and reasons to believe, demand leaks immediately.

CRO is not a "project" or just a design and UX problem. It is a function of the demand engine governed by three forces:

1. **Pricing:** Clear, consistent, competitive, and aligned across channels.
2. **Assortment:** The right products, merchandised intentionally for eCommerce demand.
3. **Convenience:** Navigation and site experience, fulfillment speed, and frictionless checkout.

When pricing and assortment are misaligned, UX improvements deliver marginal gains and false confidence.

The further down the funnel a customer moves, the more eCommerce must own the experience. Brand strategy should provide narrative and guardrails, but eCommerce should own monetization.

However, you must be cautious here. The most honest conversion metric is not conversion rate. It is dollars per visit (DPV; $/visit) because this reflects how well the system monetizes all demand, not just the easiest traffic.

> **Operating Shift:** Stop managing to conversion rate and start managing to DPV. DPV is the ultimate measure of how well your site monetizes demand. It forces you to look at the intersection of traffic, AOV, CVR, and margin. High-performing teams run a weekly conversion diagnostic that looks for friction in the PLP-to-cart journey specifically for hero products.

3. Compounding Demand (Retention and LTV)

This is where the real profit is made—and where most brands never find their groove.

A common failure is to reduce retention to email cadence (i.e., "Send more emails!"). True retention is the systematic and multiple-touch process of turning a one-time buyer into a repeat customer and, eventually, an advocate.

When the postpurchase experience is purely transactional—or worse, frustrating—the business develops a retention deficit. A healthy engine uses first-party data to build lifecycle journeys that reflect true customer behavior. It knows when a customer is likely to reorder, when they are ready to trade up, and when they are likely to leave and not come back.

As retention improves, owned revenue from email and SMS grows as a percentage of the total mix, which in turn decreases reliance on expensive paid channels. LTV then rises, and acquisition becomes scalable instead of fragile.

This is compounding demand.

Operating Shift: Build automated lifecycle journeys that map to the product's natural usage cycle. Review CRM/retention metrics and initiatives in every WBR and MBR. Ensure retention KPIs are a critical part of the monthly scorecard. The KPIs that measure this component of the demand engine are LTV, percentage of revenue from CRM, CRM list size, social follower growth, net promoter score (NPS), and customer satisfaction (CSAT). A high-performing retention system includes the following:

- The Welcome Series: Educating the customer to ensure the first experience is successful.
- The Replenishment Trigger: Reminding the customer to buy exactly when they are running low.
- The Win-Back: Identifying "at-risk" customers before they churn.

Demand Engine Nonnegotiables

Operating a demand engine requires a departure from traditional marketing silos. First, the engine must be reviewed as a single, integrated system rather than a collection of channel-level reports. This means that retention metrics must directly influence acquisition decisions. For example, if LTV is softening, the allowable CAC must contract, regardless of what the marketing dashboard claims.

In this system, DPV outranks CVR as the primary KPI of on-site success because it accounts for the commercial efficiency of the visit, not just the binary outcome of a click. Furthermore, the engine requires discipline to protect prospecting investment during volatility. When performance tightens, the natural instinct is to harvest existing demand by cutting top-of-funnel spending, but this is merely a way of borrowing growth from the future at a high interest rate. Finally, every brand investment must be held accountable for showing up downstream in search intent or direct traffic; otherwise, it is art and not engine fuel.

The engine must hold when performance tightens or when the market gets softer, not just when growth is easy and the wind is at your back.

The Rhythm of the Engine: Weekly, Monthly, Quarterly

Understanding the mechanics of the demand engine is useless without a cadence that turns insight into action. The WBR is the engine's diagnostic heartbeat. Again, it is worth emphasizing here: The WBR is not a forum for storytelling or "reporting theater" but instead must be a session for rapid-fire and near-term actionable decisions. By analyzing shifts in the traffic mix, creative fatigue, and prospecting health, the team should decide where to lean in or pull back on spending and activity in real time. Reviewing DPV and retention signals forces the team to determine where on-site friction must be fixed immediately and whether performance issues are demand, conversion, or retention problems. If a weekly meeting ends without a change to creative priorities, site-friction fixes, or media allocation, the system is failing.

The MBR shifts the focus from reaction to understanding. This is where the brand, eCommerce, finance, and operations teams align on a shared truth. By evaluating blended CAC against the plan and monitoring LTV movement by cohort, the organization can and should determine whether the funnel needs rebalancing. Brand demand indicators, such as search interest and direct traffic, help everyone stay honest about brand investments and the headwinds or tailwinds they face. The owned versus paid revenue mix analysis and conversion or retention leakage should help diagnose core issues in the demand engine that need meaningful coordinated action. This is the moment to decide whether to shift investment between brand awareness and retention or whether other adjustments are needed to counter demand signals.

During the QBR, the engine undergoes a structural audit to ensure the business is not drifting into a death spiral. This is the truth-telling session for leadership to ask the hard questions: Are we actually earning demand, or are we simply overharvesting our existing audience? Is LTV keeping pace with the rising costs of acquisition? Are brand investments showing up downstream? This quarterly rebalancing is where leadership decides whether the engine needs tuning or structural repair.

Operating Shift: Move from reporting on the past to engineering the future. Most meetings are spent explaining why the previous week's numbers happened. High-performance teams spend only 20 percent of the meeting on what happened and 80 percent on what should change. This shift requires a decision-first agenda backed by the Data → Insight → Action cycle. Instead of walking through a slide deck of charts, the meeting should begin with the three biggest deviations from the plan and end with a documented list of adjustments to spending, creative concepts, and site priorities.

The Demand Engine Scorecard

While the narrative drives the strategy, the Demand Engine Scorecard prevents the system from being managed by opinion or fear. No single metric tells the truth. The truth lies in the relationship between create, capture, and compound indicators.

- **To create demand:** We track share of search, the ratio of branded to nonbranded traffic, organic and direct traffic trends, and the "hit rate" of new creative concepts.
- **To capture demand:** We monitor blended CAC, DPV, paid traffic conversion versus site average, and the specific contribution of prospecting traffic to the total mix.
- **To compound demand:** We measure repeat rates by cohort, LTV trends, time to second purchase, and the percentage of revenue generated by owned channels.

When viewed together, these metrics reveal the health of the entire loop. You stop asking, "How is Meta performing?" and start asking, "How is the engine performing?"

Operating Shift: Move from siloed KPIs to systemic ratios. A single metric in isolation can be a lie. A high ROAS is a victory if it's driven by new customer acquisition, but it's a warning sign if it's merely the result of overtargeting your existing customers. To run a true engine, you must manage the ratios between these components. If your "create" signals (search interest) are down, you should expect your "capture" costs (CAC) to rise. If your "compound" metrics (repeat rate) are strong, you can afford to be more aggressive in your acquisition spend. By shifting your focus to these interdependencies, you stop playing Whac-A-Mole with individual channel stats and start engineering the economic outcome of the entire business.

Where ROAS Fits

In the demand engine, ROAS is a thermostat, not a steering wheel.

When the engine runs hot (high CAC and low LTV), ROAS signals the problem and tells you to slow down or fix the creative assets. When the engine is efficient, ROAS confirms it and tells you to lean in. But the business is never managed to the thermostat. It is managed by fixing the components that the thermostat measures.

The fastest way to break the engine is to impose arbitrary channel-level ROAS targets. High-performing eCommerce brands manage blended economics. They understand that strong brand demand lifts direct and organic traffic, which in turn boosts paid performance and stabilizes ROAS without stifling growth.

The Death Spiral: Why Demand Engines Fail

When a brand ignores the loop, it risks entering the "demand death spiral."

This is a self-inflicted cycle in which tactical fixes cause structural damage. It begins with brand decay, which causes CACs to rise as the market loses interest. In a reflexive attempt to "save ROAS," the team cuts prospecting spend, effectively shrinking the pond of new customers. As the pond of potential new customers dries up, retention naturally drops, leaving the brand with fewer people to sell to. Desperate to hit the monthly number, the organization leans into aggressive discounting, which momentarily spikes revenue but permanently compresses margins.

The demand engine death spiral leaves the business with no capital to reinvest in the storytelling or product innovation required to fix the brand in the first place. This is not a media failure that can be solved with better ads. It is a systemic collapse that can only be reversed by managing the engine as a single, recirculating loop.

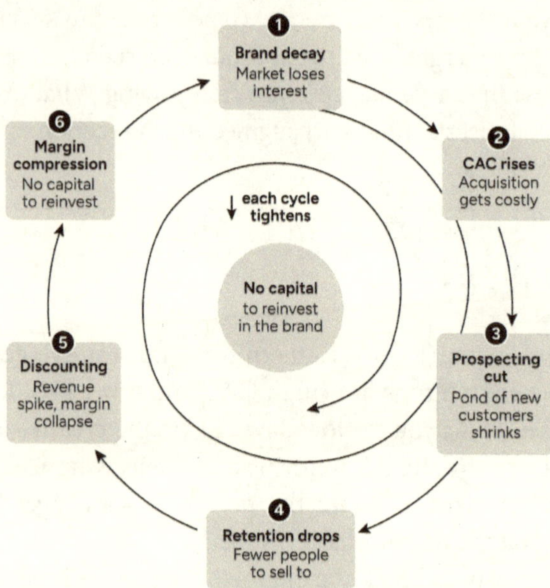

The Demand Death Spiral. Brand decay triggers rising CAC, which forces prospecting cuts, which weakens retention, which drives discounting, which compresses margins, leaving no capital to rebuild the brand, creating a negative self-reinforcing flywheel of demand.

CEO BRIEFING

- **Truth:** Acquisition is a symptom. Brand and retention are root causes. When acquisition feels broken, the issue is almost always weak storytelling or weak repeat behavior.
- **Red Flag:** If more than 80 percent of monthly revenue comes from new customers, the business is not compounding. It is operating on a high-interest loan from paid media.
- **Key Question:** "Is our demand engine earning more demand than it pays for, or is the business renting revenue?"

OPERATOR DIAGNOSTIC

Answer **Yes** or **No** to each question.

Go-to-Market

1. Do we have a unified eCommerce calendar that the brand, performance, and merchandising teams align to?
2. Is brand demand tracked through search, organic, and direct signals?
3. Is performance spend governed by CAC, LTV, and margin guardrails?

Conversion and Experience

4. Does eCommerce own lower-funnel decisions, with the brand team supplying guardrails?
5. Are pricing and promotions consistent and enforced across channels?
6. Do we manage DPV as a core KPI?

Retention and LTV

7. Is LTV measured by cohort and reviewed monthly?
8. Do lifecycle journeys exist beyond promotions?
9. Are CX insights systematically fed into CRM and merchandising?

System Health

10. Can we explain how changes in retention affect allowable CAC?
11. Do weekly and monthly reviews diagnose leakage across the loop?
12. When pressure rises, does the system tighten or fragment?

Scoring and Interpretation

Yes to 10–12 questions: Strong engine. Focus on compounding.

Yes to 6–9 questions: Functional but fragile. Expect leaks under pressure.

Yes to 0–5 questions: No demand engine. Growth depends on tactics and luck.

Summary

The demand engine is the engine of eCommerce growth. When the loop is managed deliberately, from the first brand story to the third repeat purchase, demand gets cheaper, conversion becomes predictable, and LTV compounds.

CHAPTER 15

Insight, Feedback, and Continuous Improvement

How the System Learns and Gets Stronger

If chapter 13 defined how decisions are made, and chapter 14 defined what drives growth, this chapter defines how the system learns whether those decisions are producing the desired results over time.

Most eCommerce teams believe they are data-driven. They show dashboards in meetings, circulate weekly reports, and debate KPIs. They have attribution models and analytic tools. They have more data than they know what to do with.

In reality, they are just reading numbers, not running a business. They are making decisions adjacent to data but not driven by data.

This is the biggest and most expensive trap in eCommerce: Data → Data → Data.

The result masquerades as intelligence but is just noise, and the Growth Gap widens because the organization cannot connect performance to causes, causes to decisions, or decisions to outcomes.

High-performing eCommerce organizations operate differently. They do not use data to explain the past or manipulate the data to defend opinions. They use it to run the system forward through a single operating discipline:

Data → Insight → Action → Outcome

This chapter installs that discipline as a permanent part of the eCommerce Value Chain. It also explains how continuous improvement is governed through the Growth Gap Scorecard, which measures whether the system itself is getting stronger over time.

One is the engine; the other is the diagnostic. Together, they turn information into truth and confidence.

As established in chapter 13, the eCommerce system already operates on a defined weekly, monthly, and quarterly rhythm, with clear decision forums and ownership. This chapter does not change that cadence. It defines the cognitive discipline that must operate inside it.

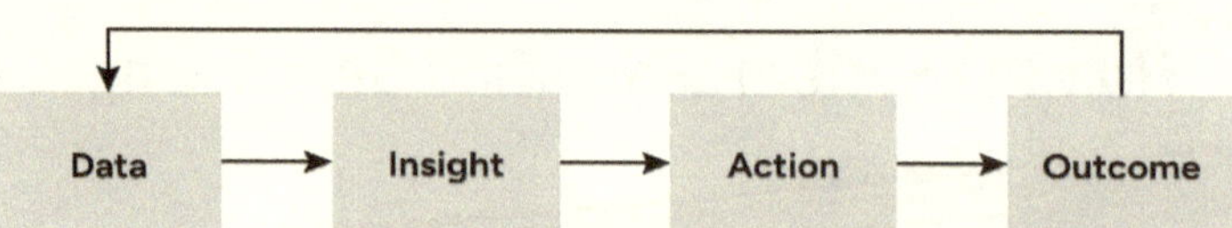

The Data → Insight → Action → Outcome Loop. The operating discipline that separates high-performing eCommerce organizations from the rest. Data is interpreted into insight, insight drives action, and action is measured against an outcome, which feeds back into the next cycle as new data. Most organizations stop at data. High performers close the loop every week.

The Nervous System of the eCommerce Business

Every scalable eCommerce organization has a nervous system, whether it is designed or accidental.

Weak systems delay, distort, or ignore signals. Pain shows up late, reactions are emotional, and the business overcorrects. In strong systems, signals are interpreted quickly, actions are deliberate, and learning compounds.

That high-performing nervous system is the Data → Insight → Action → Outcome loop.

Most teams stop at the first step. They report that conversion is down or traffic is up, but they never diagnose why. High-performance teams do not ask, "What happened?" They ask, "What changed, and why?"

They go multiple steps beyond presenting numbers to presenting truly data-driven hypotheses.

And they do not consider the loop closed until they measure the outcome against the original hypothesis. If a mobile layout is updated to improve AOV, the work is not considered done when the code goes live. It is considered done when AOV improves or does not, and the insight is memorialized.

This compounding of small, verified learnings is the operational equivalent of compound interest. A team that closes this loop fifty times a year will outpace a more talented team that does nothing but guess.

From Reporting to Diagnosis

The failure of most data systems stems from a lack of interpretation, not insufficient tools.

Unfortunately, uninterpreted data are not neutral or harmless. Such data slow decisions, fuel politics, and create false confidence. When teams cannot identify which metrics matter or how to interpret variance, three predictable failures appear:

- First, reporting masquerades as analysis. A number is presented without context, a hypothesis, or a recommended action.
- Second, "KPI-of-the-week" culture takes hold. Each week, a new metric becomes "the story," eliminating narrative consistency and preventing pattern recognition.
- Third, trust erodes. Because definitions shift and KPIs are debated, meetings devolve into arguments about accuracy instead of diagnosis.

High-performing teams eliminate this by standardizing definitions and enforcing a simple rule: No metric is discussed without a *why* and a *so what.*

> **Operating Shift:** Move from reporting on the past to diagnosing the system. This shift requires a decision-first approach to data: Never present a metric unless it is accompanied by a hypothesis (why the number moved) and a proposed action (what we will do about it). This shift changes the analyst's role from a "data puller" to a "business diagnostician," ensuring that every megabyte of data processed by the organization is aimed at a specific commercial outcome.

Installing the Loop into the Operating Rhythm

This is where learning becomes real. The Data → Insight → Action → Outcome loop must live inside the calendar. If it is optional, it will be skipped. If it is protected, it will compound.

Weekly Business Review: The Insight Forum

The WBR is a data-backed decision-making meeting. Inputs are shared in advance and focus on exceptions rather than exhaustiveness—for example, shifts in traffic mix, changes in DPV, CAC movement, signals of creative fatigue, and signals of retention movement.

The meeting itself produces decisions: one to three hypotheses explaining the variance; the actions tied to those hypotheses; and an owner, a due date, and a definition of success.

If a WBR concludes without the initiation of changes to spending, creative priorities, site-friction solutions, or lifecycle flow, it is not governance. It is a reporting theater.

Monthly Business Review: The Learning Forum

MBRs slow the system down just enough to understand it.

This is where the organization looks at cohort LTV, repeat behavior, brand demand signals, VOC themes, forecast variance, and retention health. The goal is not reaction. The goal is pattern recognition.

Monthly reviews connect upstream decisions to downstream consequences. They are where random wins become repeatable playbooks.

Quarterly Business Review: The Continuous Improvement Forum

The QBR is where learning becomes structural change.

Leadership steps back and asks harder questions: What did we learn repeatedly this quarter? What bottleneck showed up again and again? What did we fix, and what actually changed? What do we stop doing next quarter?

This is where continuous improvement becomes a discipline instead of a slogan.

Closing the Loop: Action Must Become Outcome

Most organizations take actions without recording the hypothesis, so they can never judge whether the action worked or whether it was a coincidence.

A closed loop requires discipline. For example:

- Data show that DPV dropped on the mobile platform.
- Insight suggests hero PDP engagement fell after a layout change.
- Action reverts the layout and tests a simplified module order with a bundled attachment.
- Outcome verifies whether DPV recovered within the expected window.

Only then does learning compound. Over a year, a team that closes this loop dozens of times fundamentally changes the economics of the business.

Operating Shift: Move from reporting theater to operational governance. Instead of reviewing a thirty-slide deck of what happened, the meetings should focus on the three largest variances in the system and the specific actions taken to address them. By protecting this cadence, you ensure that the organization's learning velocity is faster than the market's volatility, turning the loop into a competitive advantage.

The Truth Feed: Voice of the Customer

Quantitative data explain what happened, but VOC helps explain why.

Returns, reviews, and customer service tickets are often treated as back-office artifacts. In a high-performance system, they are strategic inputs.

Return reasons inform merchandising and claims. Customer service tickets inform UX and fulfillment priorities. Reviews inform PDP content and product education. NPS verbatims reveal promise gaps in creative content and positioning.

If VOC is not reviewed alongside performance metrics, the business becomes internally obsessed and blind to reality.

> **Operating Shift:** VOC belongs in the MBR. When a spike in returns or a dip in CSAT is treated with the same urgency as a dip in ROAS, the organization starts fixing root causes instead of masking symptoms.

Forecasting as Learning, Not Guessing

In immature systems, forecasting is a prediction exercise, and missing a forecast creates blame. In mature systems, forecasting is calibration. Variance is treated as insight before it is treated as failure.

Forecast deltas should be reviewed through the same weekly, monthly, and quarterly loop. Which assumption was wrong? Which signal was missed? Which constraint changed? What do we update in the model next month?

When forecasting is used in this way, confidence increases even when actual results diverge from projections, as the system becomes more intelligent.

Operating Shift: Move from forecasting for prediction to forecasting for calibration. In immature organizations, a missed forecast triggers a search for someone to blame; in high-performance systems, it triggers a search for an assumption to update. This shift requires treating every forecast as a collection of testable hypotheses rather than a set of fixed expectations. When you miss a target, the goal is not to "try harder" but to identify which specific variable or KPI deviated from the model. By reviewing these deltas through the Data → Insight → Action → Outcome loop, you turn financial variance into institutional intelligence. This turns the forecasting process into a sharpening stone for the entire business, ensuring that even when you miss the number, you gain the confidence that comes from a smarter system.

The Immune System: The Growth Gap Scorecard

It is important to distinguish this scorecard from the Demand Engine Scorecard introduced in chapter 14. The Demand Engine Scorecard is tactical and highly quantitative, and it measures the health of how demand is flowing through acquisition, conversion, and retention using metrics like search interest, DPV, CAC, and LTV.

The Growth Gap Scorecard is structural and more qualitative, and it measures the health of the underlying system that produces those numbers. Capabilities, infrastructure, operating rhythm, and cross-functional alignment live here. A weak system, even one with strong demand, will eventually collapse. The Growth Gap Scorecard exists to ensure the system itself is getting stronger over time.

If the weekly loop is the heartbeat, the Growth Gap Scorecard is the immune system.

While weekly and monthly rhythms govern decisions in motion, the scorecard monitors the health of the system that produces those decisions. It prevents road-map thrash and exposes structural weaknesses before they show up as financial misses.

The Growth Gap Scorecard evaluates five components from the eCommerce Value Creation System:

- Strategy and Financial Linkages
- Demand Engine
- Capabilities and Process
- Infrastructure and Operations
- eCommerce Value-Chain

Each component is scored red, yellow, or green with brief commentary.

Green does not mean perfect. Green signifies that the area is not the current bottleneck and does not require prioritized action.

Three example scorecards are included at the end of this chapter, representing early-stage, mid-maturity, and high-maturity systems respectively. They are designed to be reviewed as a set. The contrast across all three is more instructive than any single example on its own.

Integrating the Loop and the Scorecard

This is where the concepts lock together.

The weekly Data → Insight → Action → Outcome loop produces evidence. The scorecard aggregates that evidence and forces prioritization.

If weekly loops repeatedly fail to produce outcomes, the Capabilities and Process component turns red. If VOC consistently surfaces fulfillment friction, the Infrastructure and Operations component turns yellow. If brand demand signals weaken, the Demand Engine component turns red.

The scorecard is not an opinion. It is the accumulated result of learning cycles.

> **Operating Shift:** Stop treating the scorecard as status. Treat it as a funding and sequencing tool. Red and yellow components must map to initiatives, owners, timelines, and expected system impact.

What Changes When the System Learns

When an organization moves beyond dashboard theater and embraces a true culture of insight, feedback, and continuous improvement, the business undergoes a fundamental shift from fragile to durable. The first sign of this maturity is the acceleration of decision-making. Because the data is trusted and the logic is shared, the endless debates that once paralyzed the team begin to fade. Clear maturity scorecards lead to sharper investment decisions and more stable road maps as the business stops reacting to weekly fluctuations and starts building toward high-leverage outcomes.

As the system learns, financial volatility declines, and forecast confidence improves. Predictability replaces luck, and since the "why" behind the numbers is now understood, internal politics fade and cross-functional trust rises. Eventually, newfound structural health manifests in the economics of the business: The LTV:CAC ratio improves not through a single hack but through the relentless compounding of small, verified improvements. At this juncture, eCommerce transitions from a series of fires to extinguish to a machine that compounds value with each iteration.

CEO BRIEFING

- **Truth:** Data do not create clarity; interpretation does. If your team is bringing you dashboards instead of diagnoses, they are not running the business.
- **Red Flag:** If meetings debate numbers instead of producing decisions and follow-ups, the system is not learning. If the road map changes every time a major KPI dips, you lack a scorecard to anchor your strategy.
- **Key Questions:** "Are we closing the loop on our actions to see if they worked, or are we just moving from one project to the next?" and "Are we getting smarter every quarter, or are we just producing better decks?"

OPERATOR DIAGNOSTIC

Answer **Yes** or **No** to each question.

1. Do we distinguish clearly between reporting and insight?
2. Do weekly reviews produce hypotheses and decisions?
3. Are actions tied to owners, timelines, and success criteria?
4. Do we review outcomes of prior actions consistently?
5. Do we maintain a narrative across weeks and quarters?
6. Is VOC reviewed alongside performance data?
7. Is forecasting used as calibration, not blame?

8. Do scorecard reds and yellows drive road-map changes?
9. Is there a single source of truth for system health?
10. Are data trusted across the brand, eCommerce, and finance teams?

Scoring and Interpretation

Yes to 8–10 questions: The system learns and compounds.

Yes to 5–7 questions: Learning exists but is fragile.

Yes to 0–4 questions: Data are present; learning is not.

Summary

High-performing eCommerce organizations do not win because they have more data. They win because they learn faster and make it actionable.

By installing a disciplined Data → Insight → Action → Outcome loop inside weekly and monthly rhythms and governing improvement through a system-level scorecard, the business replaces noise with clarity and reactivity with confidence.

This is how the Growth Gap closes permanently.

Next, we turn learning into execution at scale with the long-term road map that sequences, funds, and sustains improvement over the next twelve to thirty-six months.

Example Growth Gap Scorecards

The following three scorecards illustrate what the Growth Gap Scorecard looks like in practice across different stages of system maturity. Each example reflects a real pattern. The red example shows a business where the system has not yet been built, so stabilization, not growth, is the priority. The yellow example shows a business with meaningful progress made but a clear primary bottleneck still constraining performance. The green example shows a system operating as designed, where the work shifts from fixing to compounding. Most eCommerce organizations will recognize themselves somewhere in this range. Many will see their current state in one scorecard and their target state in another.

Growth Gap Scorecard | Example 1: Ridgeline Outdoor Co. | Q2 2024 | Overall Status: Yellow (Mid-Maturity)

GROWTH GAP SCORECARD

Component	Status	Assessment	Priority Actions
Strategy & Financial Linkages	YELLOW	eCommerce role is defined as a growth engine, and contribution margin guardrails exist on paper. However, guardrails are inconsistently enforced. Example: Q2 promotional decisions bypassed margin floors twice without formal review. Annual plan reconciliation between eCommerce and finance remains incomplete. We have not established clear LTV:CAC thresholds.	1. Reconvene finance and eCommerce to reconcile Q3 plan assumptions. 2. Enforce margin floor review as a required gate for all promotional approvals. 3. Finance and eCommerce to establish version 1 LTV:CAC targets based on historical performance and go-forward requirements.
Demand Engine	RED	Paid media is carrying a disproportionate load. Blended CAC increased 22% YoY. Retention flows exist but are under-resourced and not governed by LTV targets. Brand demand signals are weakening (direct and organic traffic down 11% vs. prior year). Repeat Rate is stalling, and CRM list growth needs acceleration. The demand engine is manufacturing revenue, not compounding it.	1. Audit retention architecture and assign single owner with LTV accountability. 2. Establish prospecting floor decoupled from ROAS targets. 3. Review brand storytelling investment against direct traffic trends.
Capabilities & Process	YELLOW	Internal ownership is clearer than twelve months ago. eCommerce P&L owner is named and active. However, agency relationships remain loosely governed. Three active agency partners with overlapping scopes and no documented RACI. Decision rights at the campaign level are still ambiguous.	1. Document RACI for all agency partners by end of Q3. 2. Resolve campaign-level decision rights between internal team and performance agency.

Infrastructure & Operations	GREEN	Technology stack is stable and supporting current volume. Fulfillment SLAs are being met consistently. Data dictionary was finalized in Q1 and is actively used in weekly reviews. This component is not the current bottleneck.	1. Monitor peak-season capacity assumptions ahead of Q4. No major structural actions required this quarter.
eCommerce Value Chain	YELLOW	Weekly Business Review is running consistently. Monthly Business Review is inconsistent. Skipped twice in Q2 due to competing priorities. Hypothesis and Action Log exists but is not being closed out. Actions are recorded but outcomes are rarely documented. The loop is open more often than it is closed.	1. Protect MBR as a fixed calendar commitment. No cancellations without CEO approval. 2. Enforce closed-loop discipline: no new hypothesis added to the log until prior action outcome is recorded.

Overall System Status: YELLOW The business has meaningful infrastructure in place but is operating with an open demand engine leak and inconsistent operating discipline. The Demand Engine is the primary bottleneck. Until CAC is brought back within guardrails and retention is governed by LTV targets, scaling investment will widen the Growth Gap rather than close it.

Q3 Sequencing Priority: Demand Engine (RED) → Strategy & Financial Linkages (YELLOW) → eCommerce Value Chain (YELLOW)

Growth Gap Scorecard | Example 2: Cascade Athletic | Q3 2024 | Overall Status: Green (High Maturity)

GROWTH GAP SCORECARD

Component	Status	Assessment	Priority Actions
Strategy & Financial Linkages	GREEN	eCommerce role is clearly defined as a profit center with explicit contribution margin floors governing all promotional and paid media decisions. Annual plan was reconciled across eCommerce, brand, and finance in January with no outstanding gaps. Two proposed Q3 campaigns were modified before launch to meet margin requirements.	1. Begin Q4 planning reconciliation no later than mid-October to protect holiday guardrails. 2. No structural changes required this quarter.
Demand Engine	GREEN	Blended CAC declined 14% YoY while revenue grew 19%. Retention architecture is fully operational. Behavioral triggers covering replenishment, win-back, and post-purchase education are active. Direct and organic traffic up 17% vs. prior year, reflecting compounding brand equity investment. The demand engine is earning revenue, not manufacturing it.	1. Evaluate prospecting budget increase for Q4 given demonstrated CAC efficiency. 2. Audit win-back flow performance ahead of holiday lapse window.
Capabilities & Process	YELLOW	Internal ownership is clear and P&L accountability is functioning well. Primary gap: the performance creative function is dependent on a single internal resource with no documented succession or agency backup. This creates key-person risk that could disrupt creative velocity during peak season or in the event of a personnel change.	1. Document performance creative workflow so a second resource can execute without tribal knowledge. 2. Identify and brief a backup creative partner before November 1.

Infrastructure & Operations	GREEN	Technology stack is stable and well-integrated. Fulfillment SLAs exceeded targets for the third consecutive quarter. Data infrastructure is clean. Shared data dictionary enforced across finance, eCommerce, and marketing. Peak-season capacity confirmed with the 3PL partner.	1. Confirm Q4 inventory positioning with merchandising by October 15. 2. No structural actions required.
eCommerce Value Chain	GREEN	Weekly and monthly reviews are running consistently with no cancellations in Q3. The Hypothesis and Action Log is actively maintained. 34 closed loops in the quarter with outcomes documented and reviewed at the MBR. Forecast accuracy improved for the third consecutive quarter.	1. Formalize the Q3 Learning Library before Q4 ramp begins. Protect institutional knowledge from holiday-season context switching. 2. No cadence changes required.

Overall System Status: GREEN (High Maturity). The system is operating as designed. Economics are governed, demand is compounding, the operating rhythm is protected, and the organization is learning consistently. The single yellow (key-person risk in the creative function is a contained, addressable risk rather than a structural constraint. It should be resolved before Q4 peak to protect creative velocity.

Q4 Sequencing Priority: Capabilities & Process (Yellow: resolve before peak) → Sustain and compound all Green components.

Growth Gap Scorecard | Example 3: Harrow & Finch Home Goods | Q1 2024 | Overall Status: Red (Early Stage / Distressed)

GROWTH GAP SCORECARD

Component	Status	Assessment	Priority Actions
Strategy & Financial Linkages	RED	No documented eCommerce role exists. Leadership has described eCommerce as both a growth engine and a brand awareness channel in the same quarter without reconciling the implications of each. Contribution margin is not tracked at the eCommerce channel level. Two teams are operating from different revenue figures with no reconciliation process in place.	1. Declare and document the strategic role of eCommerce. One definition, approved by CEO and CFO. 2. Establish a shared contribution margin model within 30 days. No major spend decisions until this exists. 3. Reconcile revenue definitions between finance and eCommerce immediately.
Demand Engine	RED	Paid media represents 71% of total eCommerce revenue. Blended CAC increased 38% YoY with no corresponding improvement in LTV. No retention architecture exists beyond a monthly promotional email. Direct and organic traffic represent less than 12% of sessions. The business is entirely dependent on paid spend and has no compounding demand in place.	1. Do not increase paid spend until CAC guardrails are defined and margin math is confirmed. 2. Assign a single owner to retention with a 90-day mandate to install minimum viable lifecycle flows. 3. Add direct and organic traffic as a standing metric in all weekly reviews.
Capabilities & Process	RED	No single owner of the eCommerce P&L. Four agency partners are active with overlapping scopes, no RACI, and no documented decision rights. The performance agency is making spend decisions without margin visibility. Internal team bandwidth is consumed by agency management and reporting rather than strategic direction.	1. Name a single eCommerce P&L owner within two weeks. Make it public and unambiguous. 2. Conduct an agency scope audit; consolidate or eliminate overlapping partners. 3. Restrict agency spend authority until margin guardrails are in place.

Infrastructure & Operations	YELLOW	Technology stack is functional and not the primary constraint. Fulfillment SLAs are being met at adequate levels. Primary gap is data: no shared data dictionary exists, metric definitions vary by team, and reporting tools produce conflicting outputs.	1. Prioritize data dictionary creation as a Phase 1 task. 2. No platform or fulfillment changes until red components are stabilized.
eCommerce Value Chain	RED	No formal Weekly Business Review exists. Performance is reviewed ad hoc in response to crises. No Monthly Business Review cadence. No Hypothesis and Action Log. Decisions are made verbally, undocumented, and rarely followed up on. The organization has no institutional memory of what it has tried, what worked, or why.	1. Install a Weekly Business Review immediately. 60 minutes, fixed day, mandatory attendance. 2. Begin a Hypothesis and Action Log in a shared document. Complexity can come later; the habit must start now. 3. Cancel all ad hoc status meetings and replace with the WBR.

Overall System Status: RED (Early Stage / Distressed). The system is not functioning. There is no shared truth, no single owner, no operating rhythm, and no compounding demand. The business is manufacturing revenue through paid spend without the economic visibility to know whether that revenue is creating or destroying value. Scaling investment in this state will accelerate the Growth Gap, not close it. The immediate priority is stabilization.

Q2 Sequencing Priority: Strategy & Financial Linkages (define role, build margin model) → eCommerce Value Chain (install WBR) → Capabilities & Process (name owner, consolidate agencies) → Demand Engine (govern CAC before scaling) → Infrastructure & Operations (data dictionary).

CHAPTER 16

Implementing the System Without Breaking the Business

Sequencing, Maturity, and Leadership Behavior

Part 3 of this book is comprehensive by design. It is a proven system, not a set of tips. But comprehensiveness triggers a common reaction inside most brands: overload. Leaders see the whole machine at once and perhaps conclude it is unrealistic. Teams might see the workload and assume it means more meetings, more decks, and more pressure.

Getting overwhelmed before starting is how transformations die an early death.

This system requires the same implementation discipline as any durable operation. Focus on sequencing, maturing capability over time, and protecting operating discipline long enough for compounding to take hold.

This chapter bridges the understanding of the eCommerce Value-Creation System and its adoption into your business by making part 3 usable.

The Real Risk: Initiative Chaos

Most brands do not fail at closing the Growth Gap because they lack ideas. They fail because they cannot sequence the work.

They treat every initiative as equally urgent, start too much at once, layer new tools on top of broken processes, and chase "easy wins" that do not fix root causes. They allow new opinions to hijack priorities midquarter. Then they ultimately confuse motion with progress.

Their road map eventually becomes a graveyard of scattered projects, political negotiations, pet ideas, half-finished initiatives, and shiny objects that change the moment a new fire breaks out or a new tool is pitched. Initiative chaos substitutes for a strategic plan.

A real road map does something fundamentally different. It converts the Growth Gap Scorecard diagnosis into a disciplined, prioritized sequence of system improvements. It tells the organization not just what to do, but what to do first and why.

If you take nothing else from this chapter, take this: Complexity becomes the enemy only when priority and sequence are absent.

The Road-Map Principles That Prevent Overwhelm

In a high-performing eCommerce business, the road map is not just a document you possess. It is a discipline you run. Initiative chaos happens when teams attempt to scale before the fundamentals are stable. They add spending before they have clarity on the contribution margin. They launch new marketing channels before they have creative velocity. They redesign sites before pricing and assortment are aligned. They buy new technology tools before they have the discipline to use them.

Here's the persistent eCommerce myth that needs to be busted: High performance comes from doing the right things in the right order, not from doing more. The overarching principle of closing the Growth Gap is simple but not easy: maturity before scale.

Maturity improvement happens in layers. First, stabilize economics and truth so that decisions are based on shared math and not internal politics. Next, build a repeatable operating discipline so that the business reliably learns from its actions. Only then should you scale the demand systems. Finally, build depth in capabilities and infrastructure to ensure the system withstands volatility.

A road map is not the same as a backlog. A backlog is a passive list of work and unvetted ideas. A road map is a sequenced plan designed specifically to close the Growth Gap. It forces trade-offs, protects focus, and links every initiative to a measurable economic or systemic outcome.

Sequencing is not complicated, but it is usually unpopular because it requires saying "not yet" to genuinely good ideas. The correct road-map hierarchy is strict:

- Red scorecard indicators come first. Fix the break points before you chase growth.
- Fundamentals come before tools. Do not automate broken processes.
- Truth comes before velocity. Lock in definitions and guardrails before you accelerate activity.
- Loops come before leverage. Protect operating discipline before you scale the demand engine.

> **Operating Shift:** Move from project hoarding to a sequenced maturity-improvement approach. Skipping layers of maturity creates technical debt in the operating model. Enforce a red-to-green hierarchy: No new capability or channel gets funded until the red items are contained.

What Not to Do in the First Ninety Days

The fastest way to break the business is to confuse early momentum with major change. In the first ninety days, avoid anything that multiplies complexity before the foundation holds.

Do not re-platform. Do not run an organizational redesign. Do not start an agency search as a proxy for strategy. Do not launch a loyalty program. Do not initiate an attribution rebuild that becomes a months-long detour. Rule of thumb: If it increases moving parts before you have shared math, shared definitions, a shared plan, and clear ownership, it can wait.

A Growth Gap Road Map in Four Phases

Closing the Growth Gap goes beyond a single quarterly initiative. It is an ongoing and multiphased maturity progression. The timeline that follows reflects how durable systems are built, layer by layer, with each phase reinforcing the one before it.

The phases intentionally overlap. Some capabilities begin in one phase and deepen in the next. The objective is not to follow this like a rigid script but to focus on the order of operations. When you skip layers, you create technical debt in the operating model. When you sequence correctly, momentum compounds.

The timeline suggested here (twenty-four months) reflects a realistic pace for most mid-market brands starting from a fragmented state. But it is not a hard rule. Brands with stronger foundations may move through the early phases in weeks rather than months. What does not change is the sequence. Phase 1 must precede Phase 2. Phase 2 must precede Phase 3. A brand that enters this work with clean economics, shared truth, and clear ownership can compress the timeline significantly, but it cannot skip the layers. The phases hold regardless of how fast you move through them.

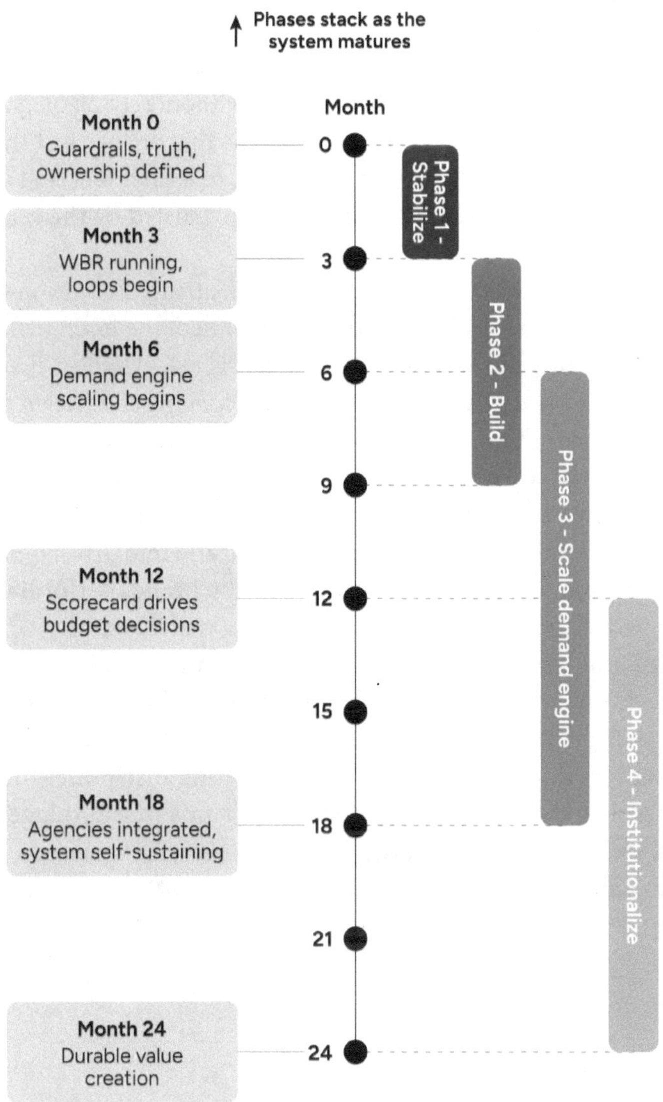

The Growth Gap Road Map. Four overlapping phases build on one another in sequence: Stabilize the business, Build repeatable execution, Scale the demand engine , and Institutionalize high performance. Phases overlap intentionally, and sequencing correctly is what allows momentum to compound.

Phase 1: Stabilize the Business (Months 0–3)

In this first phase, the objective is stability, not growth. You are building a system that can make high-stakes decisions without relying on guesswork.

Start by establishing economic guardrails that are not just theoretical but defined and enforced. Define CAC limits, margin floors, and allowable discount depth, backed by contribution logic trusted by the finance and eCommerce teams.

Then stabilize the company's version of the truth. Reach consensus on what counts as revenue, how returns are handled, the exact definition of new versus returning, and how profitability is calculated in eCommerce terms. If the marketing and finance teams are looking at different numbers, the business cannot improve, and instead, teams will only argue.

Next, resolve ownership. In immature systems, accountability is diffused. Everyone is responsible for the P&L, which means no one is. Move away from committee-based decision-making and into driver and support roles. You cannot stabilize a system when the brand, performance, and finance teams are operating under conflicting mandates.

With guardrails, definitions, and owners in place, identify the real bottleneck—not the loudest problem in the room but the key constraints limiting performance.

Finally, install a minimum viable operating discipline—the single, protected weekly and monthly decision forums that produce actions, owners, and outcomes. Resist the urge to fix everything at once. The goal is alignment and traction. Trying to rebuild the entire machine in month one erodes trust and burns the team.

Operating Shift: To move from chaos to traction in the first ninety days, focus on the rules of the game before the playbook:

1. **Draft the Financial Manifesto:** Sit with the finance team to sign off on a single-page document defining your contribution margin logic and red-line CAC limits. This prevents midquarter panic when performance fluctuates.
2. **Define the Single Point of Accountability:** Decide who owns the eCommerce P&L and make it clear to the organization. For every component on the scorecard, name one person as the driver. If you have two people sharing a KPI, you have zero people responsible for it.
3. **Audit the Vocabulary:** Create a data dictionary that defines every key metric. If the marketing and finance teams are looking at different revenue numbers, stop all other work until this is reconciled.
4. **Appoint a Bottleneck Owner:** Identify the one component on your scorecard that is the primary constraint and assign it a lead who reports on progress weekly.
5. **Audit the Calendar:** Cancel every recurring status-update meeting. Replace them with one sixty-minute WBR that follows the Data → Insight → Action → Outcome loop.

Phase 2: Build Repeatable Execution (Months 3–9)

Once guardrails and truth are stable, the focus needs to shift from stabilization to repeatability. This is where the business builds the muscle that makes future investments pay off. The goal is to move the Data → Insight → Action → Outcome loop from an aspirational idea into a daily reality.

The team should shift from reading the news to diagnosing the business. Meetings should stop being recaps and start being investigations. The MBR should become the place where the organization slows down just enough to connect upstream decisions to downstream consequences.

This is also where the customer's voice becomes a real operating input and site optimization moves away from subjective design debate to commercial decision-making grounded in DPV.

This phase often looks "small" compared to big projects like re-platforming or brand relaunches. Do not be tempted to skip this phase. It is the foundation that keeps the system from collapsing under future scale.

Operating Shift: Institutionalize learning by enforcing closed loops:

1. **Install the MBR:** Set a fixed date (e.g., the fifth business day of every month) for a deep-dive session. This is not a recap of the weekly meetings. It is a search for patterns. Focus on LTV movement, forecast accuracy, and cross-functional bottlenecks.
2. **Mandate the "Why":** Enforce a rule that no performance chart can be presented in a meeting unless it is accompanied by a hypothesis. If a team member says, "Traffic is up," the immediate follow-up must be, "Based on our diagnosis, why is it up, and what is the implication for next week?"
3. **Operationalize VOC:** Move your customer feedback data into your weekly and monthly reviews. If return rates spike or sentiment dips, it must trigger a "red" status on the scorecard just as quickly as an ROAS miss would.
4. **Create a Hypothesis and Action Log:** Maintain a simple, shared log of every decision made in the WBR. It must track the initial data signal, the action taken, and most importantly, the measured outcome. Review the hits and misses of these hypotheses and actions during the MBR to build institutional intelligence.
5. **Audit Decision Criteria:** For site or creative changes, replace "I like this" with "We believe this will move [metric] by [X] because of [insight]." If the outcome doesn't match the hypothesis, document the learning before moving to the next test.

Phase 3: Scale the Demand Engine (Months 6–18)

Only after the foundation is in place and operating discipline is stable should the organization lean into the levers that scale by shifting from running campaigns to building systems.

In this phase, the performance creative work matures from a quarterly scramble into a high-velocity system fed by weekly learning. Conversion becomes a function, not a redesign project. Retention evolves from "more sends" into a lifecycle architecture that compounds the value of every customer. Prospecting gets protected as a strategic necessity, not a discretionary line item, and the business has the confidence to maintain marketing reach even when short-term performance tightens.

Operating Shift: Turn marketing functions into operational workflows:

1. **Systematize Creative Production:** Establish a weekly creative-to-commerce workflow. Performance data from the previous week must dictate the following week's briefs. If a certain hook or aesthetic is winning, the system should be designed to produce five variations of it immediately.
2. **Define Conversion as a Function:** Assign a dedicated lead (internal or agency) whose only KPI is DPV. They should have a permanent friction log and a weekly deployment schedule for site enhancements, moving away from the big-bang redesign cycle.
3. **Map the Lifecycle Architecture:** Audit your automated flows. If your retention strategy relies on manual blasts, replace them with behavioral triggers (replenishment, win-back, postpurchase education) that operate twenty-four seven without manual intervention.
4. **Establish a Prospecting Floor:** Set a minimum budget for top-of-funnel awareness that is decoupled from daily ROAS targets. Use your phase 1 economic guardrails to ensure this spending is sustainable, protecting the brand's long-term demand from short-term volatility.

Phase 4: Institutionalize High Performance (Months 12–24)

In the final phase, the system needs to become durable and stop depending on heroics to hit the number. This phase transitions you from fixing the business to compounding value creation.

Role clarity is stable. Agencies operate as integrated partners rather than external vendors. Infrastructure and operations shift from constraint to enabler, supporting launches, expansions, and peak demand without threatening the P&L.

The Growth Gap Scorecard evolves from a firefighting tool into a quarterly validation cycle that prevents road-map thrash and keeps leadership aligned. Most importantly, the business can explain performance and predict outcomes with increasing accuracy.

This is the shift from fragile growth to durable value creation. The company stops asking, “How do we survive this quarter?” and starts asking, “How do we get stronger every quarter?”

Operating Shift: Move from manual to durable governance:

1. **Enforce the Scorecard-to-Budget Link:** Make the scorecard a requirement for all future funding. If a department wants more budget or a new hire, the department must demonstrate how that investment moves a component from yellow to green.
2. **Institutionalize the Learning Library:** Archive the results of every closed loop from previous phases. This becomes your Playbook of Truth, preventing new hires or outside agencies from repeating old mistakes.
3. **Audit for Key Person Risk:** Ensure the system is documented well enough that if a driver leaves, the operating rhythm doesn’t stop. High performance should be a property of the organization, not an individual.
4. **Set System Improvement KPIs:** In addition to financial targets, hold leadership accountable for system health. If revenue is up but the Infrastructure and Operations component turns red, the quarter is not considered a success.

How to Sequence Work Without Politics

A road map only works when leaders enforce rules that hold under pressure. Follow these guiding principles to ensure your road map is driven by reality and not ego.

Red comes first. If the Infrastructure and Operations component is red, the organization does not have the luxury of starting a re-platform, a new agency search, and a loyalty program simultaneously. Fix the break point before adding complexity.

Single ownership is nonnegotiable, and cross-functional does not mean ownerless. Every initiative needs one accountable leader, never a committee, or the messy middle will stall.

The road map must be intentionally hard to change. Treat it like a constitution—amendable, but only through a rigorous process. Without intentional friction, you do not have a road map; you have a mood board shaped by the pressure of the week.

The filter for any new initiative is your Growth Gap Scorecard. If it cannot be tied directly to moving a component from red to yellow or from yellow to green, it does not belong on the road map yet.

Operating Shift: Turn the road map into a contract of focus:

1. **The "Red-Line" Rule:** At the start of every quarter, highlight the red component on your scorecard. Mandate that 70 percent of the road map's resources must be allocated to these areas before green component can receive any additional funding.
2. **Assign the Owner Role:** For every road-map item, use a simple RACI (responsible, accountable, consulted, and informed) model. If there isn't a single name in the "Accountable" box, the project is paused until an owner is named and empowered.
3. **Build a Dependency Map:** Before setting a launch date for a phase 3 initiative (e.g., a loyalty program), list the phase 1 and 2 requirements (e.g., data hygiene or margin clarity). If the requirements aren't green, the launch date remains TBD.

4. **Establish the Change Control Ritual:** Create a monthly fifteen-minute "road-map amendment" window. To add a new project, the proposer must present which current project of equal effort is being deleted to make room. If nothing is deleted, nothing is added.

Leadership Behavior That Sustains the System

The early phases of closing the Growth Gap will feel slower before they feel faster. With documented decisions, structured forums, and rigorous follow-ups, it is easy to mistake discipline for bureaucracy. But this is not red tape. It is the installation of repeatability. If leaders cut these disciplines the moment results tighten or the market gets volatile, the system will never gain the momentum required to compound.

Leaders will also need to change what they reward. In chaos cultures, the firefighter becomes the hero. For example, someone saves the month with a last-minute promotion or patches a broken launch over a weekend. Those efforts may be necessary sometimes, but celebrating them teaches the organization that instability is normal.

High-performing leaders reward prevention. They celebrate clean handoffs, stable planning, and closed loops that keep fires from starting.

Finally, leaders must do their part to shield the organization from shiny objects. A new tool cannot fix a broken process. A new channel cannot fix weak economics. The job is not to approve more activity; it is to protect the sequence long enough for it to work.

Operating Shift: Change the incentives:

1. **Celebrate the Non-Event:** Publicly recognize teams that hit their targets through stable, planned execution rather than last-minute scrambles. Make predictability the highest-status trait in the building.
2. **Enforce the Closed Loop in Every Meeting:** If a team member proposes a new initiative, your first question should be: "Which previous outcome gave us the insight to do this?" If they can't answer, the project doesn't move forward.

3. **The Wait and Weight Rule:** When a shiny object or "urgent" new tool is proposed, mandate a waiting period. During that time, the proposer must document which scorecard metric it will move and which existing road-map item it will replace.
4. **Measure Maturity in Reviews:** In monthly reviews, ask the team: "What did we do this month that we won't have to do manually next month?" If the answer is "nothing," you are rewarding effort rather than system improvement.

What a Good Road Map Looks Like

A road map should be simple enough for the organization to understand and strict enough for leadership to govern. It is the single source of truth for where the company invests time, capital, and attention.

At a minimum, every road-map item needs the following:

- System linkage: which part of the Value-Creation System it supports
- Single accountable owner
- Timeline and dependencies
- Expected system impact
- Scorecard linkage: which red or yellow indicator it is designed to move

Example road map entries are provided at the end of this chapter.

The resolution of your road map should match the timeline horizon. The next twelve months should be specific enough to run, with real start and stop dates. Months twelve to twenty-four should be directional, grouped into themes. Anything beyond that is just intent, not a real plan.

The Payoff: Calm, Predictable Progress

The payoff of sequenced implementation is the transition from constant emergency to calm, predictable progress. Weekly priority whiplash fades, cross-functional alignment becomes routine, and projects finish as expected because dependencies are cleared and owners are empowered.

The organization becomes less busy and more effective. Forecasting improves because assumptions are sharpened by real feedback loops. Growth becomes less volatile because it is built on reinforced fundamentals, not short-term hacks. Even during market swings, the business can explain what is happening and what it is doing about it.

That is the hallmark of high performance.

CEO BRIEFING

- **Truth:** The system will feel slower before it feels faster. If you abandon discipline during that phase, you will stay in chaos permanently.
- **Red Flag:** If priorities change midquarter without scorecard justification, you do not have a road map. You have a backlog shaped by pressure.
- **Key Question:** "Are we sequencing work to strengthen the system, or are we starting more initiatives to feel progress?"

OPERATOR DIAGNOSTIC

Answer **Yes** or **No** to each question.

1. Do we have economic guardrails that actually govern decisions?
2. Can we name the current bottleneck in the system, not just the loudest issue?
3. Do we have a scorecard that identifies reds and yellows with shared agreement?
4. Does every initiative have a single accountable owner?
5. Are dependencies mapped so that timelines are real, not optimistic?
6. Are red indicators addressed before new growth initiatives are added?
7. Is the road map difficult to change, requiring justification and approval?
8. Do monthly reviews track progress against initiatives rather than debating new priorities?
9. Do quarterly reviews adjust priorities based on scorecard movement and outcomes?

10. Do leaders protect the operating discipline when performance tightens?

Scoring and Interpretation

Yes to 8–10 questions: Disciplined implementation. The system will compound.

Yes to 5–7 questions: Good structure. Risk of drift under pressure.

Yes to 0–4 questions: High risk of initiative chaos. Fix governance first.

Summary

Part 3 is not meant to be implemented all at once. The road map is the mechanism that turns diagnosis into a plan, and leadership behavior is what keeps the plan intact long enough for it to work.

When you prioritize reds, stabilize fundamentals, and protect operating discipline, the system gets stronger every quarter. That is how you implement the eCommerce Value-Creation System without breaking the business, and it is how you turn ambition into durable, compounding performance. Discipline is not what slows this system down. It is what allows it to scale without breaking.

REFERENCE: FIRST THIRTY DAYS CEO CHECKLIST

If you are the CEO, your job in the first month is not to "run eCommerce." Your job is to remove ambiguity and protect sequencing.

1. **Sign the Financial Manifesto**
   Approve one page that defines contribution margin logic, CAC limits, discount depth guardrails, and what "profitability" means in eCommerce terms. Make it the decision standard, not a reference doc.

2. **Name the Single P&L Driver**
   Put one person on the hook for the eCommerce P&L and make it explicit across the organization. If accountability is shared, it is not accountability.

3. **Force a Single Source of Truth**
   Require the finance, eCommerce, and marketing teams to reconcile definitions of revenue, returns, new versus returning customers, and margin treatment. No road-map work moves forward until the numbers match.

4. **Declare the Red and Protect the Sequence**
   Choose the current scorecard's red bottleneck and publicly state that it is the priority. Make it clear what will not be funded or started until that red is contained.

5. **Install Change Control**
   Set the rule for road-map changes now: Any new initiative must state (a) which scorecard indicator it moves and (b) which existing initiative of equal effort gets removed. If nothing is removed, nothing is added.

REFERENCE: Road Map in Action: Two Example Entries

A road map is only as useful as the clarity of its entries. The following two examples illustrate what a well-formed road map item looks like across two different phases. One focused on stabilization, one on scaling demand.

EXAMPLE ROAD MAP ENTRIES

Element	Phase 1 Example	Phase 3 Example
Phase	Phase 1: Stabilize	Phase 3: Scale demand engine
Initiative	Establish shared contribution margin model and data dictionary	Build performance creative system for hero products
Component	Strategy & Financial Linkages	Demand Engine
Owner	eCommerce P&L owner (driver); CFO, finance lead (support)	Head of performance marketing (driver); brand director, head of eCommerce (support)
Timeline	Weeks 1–8	Months 7–12
Dependencies	Finance and eCommerce aligned on revenue definition; CFO approval of margin floor logic	Global eCommerce calendar approved; hero product priorities confirmed by merchandising; brand narrative guardrails documented
Scorecard link	Strategy & Financial Linkages moves from Red to Yellow	Demand Engine: creative hit rate and prospecting efficiency move from Yellow to Green
Expected impact	Shared math that governs all future decisions; eliminates midquarter debates over conflicting numbers	Higher creative throughput and faster iteration; lower blended CAC through improved relevance; reduced dependency on promotions to drive volume

Note: Phase 1 entries are measured in weeks because speed to shared truth is the objective. Phase 3 entries span months because building a compounding demand system requires sustained execution, not a sprint.

CHAPTER 17

The Growth Gap Operating Kit

A Practical Reference for Running the System

This chapter on the Growth Gap Operating Kit makes the eCommerce Value-Creation System usable under pressure.

When results tighten, leaders do not need more theory. They need a clear mental model, a small set of governing tools, and unambiguous operating rules. The Growth Gap Operating Kit distills part 3 into a practical reference leaders can return to when decisions must be made quickly and confidence must be preserved.

Downloadable versions of the tools in this kit, including the scorecards and road map entry template, are available at toolkit.ecommercegrowthgap.com.

1. The Five Forces

What breaks performance

The Five Forces diagnose why eCommerce performance fails even when teams are talented, active, and well resourced.

- **Strategy Gap:** Direction is unclear or contradictory. eCommerce is asked to be everything at once, so it becomes nothing specific.

- **Financial Linkages Gap:** Revenue targets exist without contribution logic. ROAS replaces unit economics, and growth destroys value.
- **Capability and Organizational Gap:** Accountability is diffused. Decisions stall or escalate because no one truly owns outcomes.
- **Infrastructure and Process Gap:** Speed and feedback break down. Learning cycles slow until insight becomes irrelevant.
- **Demand-Generation Gap:** The business rents revenue instead of earning demand. CAC rises faster than LTV.

Role in closing the Growth Gap: The forces reveal where the system is broken so that fixes can target root causes, not symptoms.

2. The eCommerce Value-Creation System

What replaces fragmentation

The eCommerce Value-Creation System is the operating model that resolves the Five Forces by design. It connects strategy, economics, ownership, execution, and learning.

- **Foundation:** The eCommerce Value Chain
- **Four Pillars:**
  1. Strategy & Financial Linkages
  2. Demand Engine
  3. Capabilities & Process
  4. Infrastructure & Operations
- **Two Beams:**
  1. Profitable Growth
  2. Operational Excellence
- **Roof:** Value creation

Role in closing the Growth Gap: Replaces disconnected activity with an operating system that turns effort into predictable results.

3. The eCommerce Value Chain

How strategy becomes repeatable execution and learning

The eCommerce Value Chain is not an organizational chart or a process map. It is the operating logic that governs how inputs become outcomes.

It runs through cadence:

- Weekly execution and diagnosis
- Monthly understanding and alignment
- Quarterly adjustment and reallocation
- Annual strategic and operational planning

Role in closing the Growth Gap: Eliminates handoff failure by managing the business as one continuous system instead of isolated functions.

4. Strategy, Economics, and Planning as One System

How direction enters the machine

Planning works only when ambition and constraints arrive together.

Core mechanisms:

- Explicit declaration of the eCommerce role
    - Growth engine
    - Profit center
    - Brand temple
- Contribution margin guardrails
- Bottom-up KPI reality checks
- Strategic gap log to reconcile ambition with math

Role in closing the Growth Gap: Prevents deferred failure by forcing reconciliation before execution begins.

5. Ownership, Governance, and Operating Rhythm

How alignment holds under pressure

High performance does not come from organizational design. It comes from decision rights and cadence.

Key mechanisms:

- Driver and support model for decision authority
- Single accountable owner for each outcome
- WBR (decisions, not reporting)
- MMR (learning, not reaction)
- QBR (sequencing, not thrash)
- S&OP integration so that inventory and demand match

Role in closing the Growth Gap: Replaces heroics and escalation with speed, clarity, and repeatability.

6. The Demand Engine

Where growth comes from

The demand engine is a loop, not a funnel.

Three stages:

1. **Create Demand:** Brand storytelling and performance creative concepts that earn attention.
2. **Capture Demand:** Conversion systems that monetize traffic efficiently.
3. **Compound Demand:** Retention and lifecycle systems that increase LTV.

Core principles:

- CAC is governed by LTV, not ROAS targets.
- DPV replaces conversion rate as the truth metric.

- Retention is economic leverage, not email volume.
- Prospecting must be protected during volatility.

Role in closing the Growth Gap: Turns growth from rented revenue into compounding enterprise value.

7. The Two Scorecards

How health is measured

The Demand Engine Scorecard (the Pond)

Measures tactical demand health.

- Create: Search interest, direct traffic, creative hit rate
- Capture: Blended CAC, DPV, conversion efficiency
- Compound: LTV, repeat rate, owned revenue mix

The Growth Gap Scorecard (the House)

Measures structural system health and continuous improvement.

- Strategy and financial linkages
- Demand engine
- Capabilities and process
- Infrastructure and operations
- Value chain execution

Role in closing the Growth Gap: Prevents short-term wins from masking long-term decay. Ensures the system improves, not just the numbers.

8. The Data → Insight → Action → Outcome Loop

How the system learns

Learning only compounds when loops close.

Required discipline:

- No metric without a hypothesis
- No action without a defined outcome
- No outcome without documented learning

Where it lives:

- Weekly diagnosis
- Monthly pattern recognition
- Quarterly structural correction

Role in closing the Growth Gap: Increases learning velocity so that the business improves faster than the market changes.

9. The Road Map

How change is sequenced

A road map is not a backlog. It is a contract of focus.

Rules that matter:

- Red indicators first
- Fundamentals before tools
- Loops before leverage
- Single owner per initiative
- Explicit dependencies
- Hard change control

Every road-map item must include the following:

- Growth Gap component linkage
- Accountable owner
- Timeline and dependencies
- Scorecard movement
- Expected system impact

Role in closing the Growth Gap: Prevents initiative chaos and ensures progress compounds instead of resetting.

10 Leadership Behaviors That Make the System Stick

What leaders must do differently

The system breaks when leaders react emotionally under pressure.

Nonnegotiable behaviors:

- Protect cadence when results tighten.
- Reward prevention, not firefighting.
- Enforce closed loops before approving new work.
- Say no to shiny objects that violate sequence.
- Celebrate predictability over heroics.

Role in closing the Growth Gap: Turns high performance from an effort problem into a leadership standard.

11. The Nonnegotiable Tool Set

The minimum operating infrastructure for high performance

Strategy and Direction Tools

These tools prevent ambiguity before it enters the system.

- **Global Brand Strategic Marketing Calendar:** Declares the brand narratives, themes, and emphasis over time. This is the upstream signal that aligns product, inventory, and demand planning.
- **Brand Themes and Priorities:** A concise articulation of the three to four dominant stories the brand will tell this year. Prevents reactive campaign churn and narrative dilution.
- **Consumer Persona Definitions:** Clear, current definitions of the customers the brand serves, what they value, and how they decide. These are operating inputs, not marketing artifacts.
- **Brand Style and Standards Guide:** Defines guardrails for voice, design, and claims. Brand governs through standards, not approvals.

Planning and Economic Truth Tools

These tools ensure that ambition and constraints enter the machine together.

- **Financial Manifesto:** A one-page declaration of contribution margin logic, CAC limits, discount depth guardrails, and what "profitable growth" means in eCommerce terms.
- **Annual Operating Budget and Plan:** The reconciled output of top-down intent and bottom-up reality.
- **Annual KPI and Revenue Plan by Week:** Forces realism into forecasting and exposes risk early. Prevents surprise shortfalls and panic-driven decisions.
- **eCommerce P&L:** A channel-level view of revenue, contribution margin, and EBITDA that the finance and eCommerce teams both trust.

- **Strategic Gap Log:** A documented record of where top-down intent conflicts with bottom-up reality and how each gap was resolved.

Execution and Governance Tools

These tools replace consensus and escalation with ownership and cadence.

- **Global eCommerce Go-to-Market Calendar:** The single source of truth for launches, promotions, campaigns, and priorities. Aligns the brand, performance, merchandising, and operations teams.
- **eCommerce Accountability and Collaboration Map:** Defines driver and support roles across the value chain. This replaces organizational chart confusion with decision clarity.
- **Weekly Business Review (WBR):** The primary decision forum. Diagnoses execution, assigns actions, and adjusts levers in real time.
- **Weekly Dashboard:** A concise, standardized view of leading indicators. Inputs are reviewed before meetings so that decisions can be made at meetings.
- **Monthly Strategic Review (MBR):** The learning forum. Connects actions to outcomes, surfaces patterns, and informs road-map adjustments.

Measurement and Learning Tools

These tools ensure the system improves, not just performs.

- **Data Dictionary and Metric Definitions:** A shared definition of revenue, returns, new versus returning customers, CAC, LTV, DPV, and margin math. If this is not aligned, no other tool works.
- **Hypothesis and Action Log:** A running record of every decision made, the hypothesis behind it, the action taken, and the measured outcome. This is how learning compounds instead of resetting.
- **360-Degree Demand Engine Scorecard:** Measures the health of create, capture, and compound demand. This is how growth is governed.

- **Growth Gap Scorecard (Business Maturity):** Measures the health of the system itself, including strategy, economics, capabilities, infrastructure, and rhythm. This is how fragility is prevented.

Sequencing and Change Control Tools

These tools protect focus and compounding.

- Growth Gap Road Map
- A sequenced plan tied directly to scorecard movement. Every initiative has an owner, dependencies, and a system-level outcome.

How to Use This Kit

- CEOs: Use this to govern, not to manage.
- Operators: Use this to align decisions and defend focus.
- Boards: Use this to evaluate system health, not just results.

If you are unsure what to do next, return to these three questions:

1. Where is the system red?
2. What sequence protects compounding?
3. What decision removes ambiguity right now?

This is how the Growth Gap closes in practice.

Summary

You now have a complete diagnostic and operating system for closing the Growth Gap, built around sequencing, governance, and compounding execution. The only variable left is whether the organization protects the discipline long enough for it to mature.

To close the Growth Gap, endurance and repeatability trump intensity every time.

From here, the work is simple to describe and hard to do: Lead the system, enforce the sequence, and make compounding the standard.

CONCLUSION

Running the System That Wins Over Time

One last time: The eCommerce Growth Gap stems from a missing system, not missing ambition, talent, or effort.

Brands expect growth because the channel feels modern, measurable, and controllable. They assume the right website, the right agency, the right people, or the right technology will unlock performance. When results stall, they respond by increasing activity, adding more tools, and increasing pressure.

That approach does not fail loudly. It fails quietly.

The business gets busier. The decks get longer. The conversations get more detailed. But the fundamentals do not improve. The Growth Gap widens slowly, then drastically, until the organization works harder each year without making meaningful progress.

This book exists to prevent that outcome. Not by offering tactics or prescribing hacks but by installing the system that drives high-performance eCommerce. This framework aligns performance with potential, ensuring growth strengthens the business rather than strains it. It is a philosophy that treats demand as an engine rather than a collection of channels, replacing opinion with insight and activity with outcomes. By turning learning into leverage, it creates the compounding advantage that separates market leaders from the rest of the pack.

The Growth Gap closes when an organization moves beyond a single initiative or one great quarter and into a robust system of learning faster, making better decisions, and executing with discipline over time. When this system is in place, something fundamental changes. Decisions get easier, road maps stabilize rather than thrash, and meetings produce action rather than arguments. Teams finally finish what they start, forecasts become explainable, and volatility becomes manageable. In short, the business stops reacting and starts running.

High-performance eCommerce organizations are defined by control. They control their economics, their priorities, and their learning. These brands move deliberately, protecting the sequence of maturation and fixing root causes before chasing upside. They are unstoppable because they move well *and* fast.

You now have the operating system to do the same.

You can see the business clearly and diagnose the real bottlenecks. You know how to measure system health, sequence work, and scale demand without breaking your margins. Most importantly, you know how to lead the system when the pressure is highest.

This book does not promise that the work will be easy. However, the work will be worthwhile because it compounds. The Growth Gap is not your fate, nor is it a market or talent problem. It is a system problem. And systems can be built.

Brands that commit to this discipline will stand apart from competitors. They will invest with confidence, grow with discipline, and build durable enterprise value. They will turn eCommerce from a source of friction into a strategic engine that strengthens the entire business.

Their eCommerce performance will finally match their potential.

eCommerce does not reward effort. It rewards systems. And now, you know how to build them.

ABOUT THE AUTHOR

Jason Pawloski is one of the most respected voices in eCommerce and a leading architect of system-level eCommerce transformation. He has shaped the strategies, operating systems, and financial models behind some of the most successful brands in footwear, apparel, furniture, electronics, and sporting goods. His frameworks have become the reference point for how companies understand—and close—the eCommerce Growth Gap.

Jason's core belief is simple and increasingly influential: eCommerce performance isn't a marketing challenge. It's a systems challenge.

Brands don't fall behind because they lack effort, creativity, or technology. They fall behind because their strategy, economics, capabilities, infrastructure, and operating rhythm aren't aligned. Jason's work has helped redefine how organizations think about eCommerce maturity, financial linkages, demand generation, and the organizational capabilities required to compete.

Drawing from more than two decades of leading and rebuilding eCommerce businesses, Jason brings a rare combination of operator experience, analytical rigor, and systems thinking. He has guided founders, CEOs, boards, and private equity teams through transformations that turn reactive eCommerce functions into profitable, predictable, scalable growth engines. His influence is evident in how brands now talk about economics, contribution margin, and the role of eCommerce inside the broader commercial ecosystem.

Jason's career centers on the exact problem this book exposes: even with the right playbook, eCommerce teams often lack the capabilities and operating discipline to execute at a high level. His approach has consistently given brands the senior leadership, system design, and execution capability they need to accelerate performance and exceed category benchmarks.

In an industry full of tactics, trends, and short-term fixes, Jason stands out for offering something rare: a complete, coherent system for how an eCommerce business unit works and how to make it work at the highest level.

Connect and learn more about working with Jason at JasonPawloski.com.

The Growth Gap Toolkit

Everything you need to implement the system in this book is available in one place. The toolkit includes the Growth Gap Scorecard, example P&L, CEO First 30 Day Checklist, and more.

Visit toolkit.ecommercegrowthgap.com to access all resources.

Reader's Guide: Everything you need to close your Ecommerce Growth Gap - Scan to access guides, templates & tool - all in one place

www.ingramcontent.com/pod-product-compliance
Lightning Source LLC
LaVergne TN
LVHW100527110826
845146LV00002B/800

* 9 7 9 8 9 9 4 6 1 9 4 2 1 *